SIGNALLING IN THE AGE OF STEAM

Michael A. Vanns

Ian Allan
Publishing

First published 1995

ISBN 0 7110 2350 6

© Michael A. Vanns 1995

Published by Ian Allan Publishing

an imprint of Ian Allan Ltd, Terminal House,
Station Approach, Shepperton, Surrey
TW17 8AS.
Printed by Ian Allan Printing Ltd,
Coombelands House, Coombelands Lane,
Addlestone, Weybridge, Surrey KT15 1HY.

Front cover: **Ex-GWR 'Castle' No 7007**
***Great Western* waits at Oxford with the
1.45pm Paddington-Worcester train on
29 September 1956. *R. C. Riley***

Back cover: **Leicester North Junction.
*Author***

Previous page:
**Traditional Signalling. An undated
photograph of Sydenham Hill signalbox on
the London, Chatham & Dover
Railway. *Southern Railway***

CONTENTS

D0287130

s .... As such it is a companion volume to Stanley Hall's BR Signalling Handbook (Ian Allan 1992) which deals with modern forms of train control.

Although it has proved difficult, the emphasis in this book is on the typical and commonplace, not the experimental and unique. The keywords are evolution and tradition. Virtually no new form of signalling was 'invented'. Equipment, procedures and Rules & Regulations evolved over a period of time to form traditional ways of operation. The mechanical and electrical equipment, and many of the principles familiar to every signalman in the 1890s, were based on designs and principles going back to the 1860s, and any signalman of the 1890s walking into almost any signalbox anywhere in the country in the 1960s, would have been familiar with its operation.

If there is a bias in this book, then it is towards the secrets of the signalbox. Of the many and varied working environments that industry created over the years, there were few as special as that of a signalbox, large or small, busy or quiet. More people have seen and photographed outdoor signalling equipment, than have experienced the unique private world of the signalbox; this book will help to redress the balance.

Opposite:
The 70 lever McKenzie & Holland frame in Thorpe-le-Soken signalbox on the ex-GER. The levers display LNER plastic description plates. On the block shelf the illuminated diagram is an LNER standard type, whilst next to it is a Tyer's one-wire two-position 'flap' block instrument. *BR*

Following page:
Dalston Junction signalbox built by the North London Railway in 1872, controlled these two centrally-pivoted semaphores, erected in this unusual way so they could be seen from beneath the station awning and footbridge. *BR (London Midland Region)*

Left:
The GWR equivalent of the NLR semaphores at Dalston Junction, used in restricted spaces like here at High Wycombe station. *G. Boyes*

ACKNOWLEDGEMENTS AND BIBLIOGRAPHY

The author is grateful to the following who helped in the preparation of this book: for reading and vetting the text — Peter Jordan, Exeter West Group, and Richard Foster, Signalling Record Society; for creating the diagrams — Michael Worthington, Archaeology Unit, Ironbridge Gorge Museum; David Postles, Kidderminster Railway Museum & Severn Valley Railway; Stuart Atkinson, Railtrack S&T; David Houlston; Peter Waller, Ian Allan; Donald Powell; Ironbridge Gorge Museum Trust; National Railway Museum Library and Photographic Archive; Ray Towell, National Railway Museum.

Much of the detailed information has been gleaned from articles published in The Signalling Record, the journal of the Signalling Record Society, and its predecessor the Newsletter. At the time of writing the Record is edited by Jerry Plane, 6 Whitestone Road, Halesowen, West Midlands B63 3PU. The Society was formed in 1969, and provides a forum for the study of railway signalling. It can supply members with copies of track layouts, and other signalling publications not generally available to the public. Wherever possible I have used the Society's preferred terminology, and I am indebted to all those Society members who actively research and publish their findings. Anyone wishing to join the Society should write to The Membership Secretary, c/o Gribdae Cottage, Kirkcudbright DG6 4QD.

Along with original Patent Specifications, company Rules & Regulations books, appendices to working timetables, etc and other miscellaneous articles, the following were the main works referred to in the writing of this book:

Danger Ahead, the dramatic story of railway signalling, Richard Blythe, Newman Neame, 1951
Rule Book, British Railways, reprinted with amendments, Railway Clearing House, 1961
Regulations for Train Signalling and Signalmen's General Instructions, British Railways, Railway Clearing House, 1960
A Pictorial Record of LNWR Signalling, Richard D. Foster, OPC, 1982
Danger Signals, Stanley Hall, Ian Allan, 1987
Danger on the Line, Stanley Hall, Ian Allan, 1989
BR Signalling Handbook, Stanley Hall, Ian Allan, 1992
British Railway Signalling, G. M. Kitchenside & Alan Williams, Ian Allan, 1963
The Application of Electricity to Railway Working, W. E. Langdon, E. & F. N. Spon, 1897
A Pictorial Record of LNER Constituent Signalling, A. A. Maclean, OPC, 1983
Fifty Years of Railway Signalling, O. S. Nock, The Institution of Railway Signal Engineers, 1962
British Railway Signalling, O. S. Nock, George Allen & Unwin Ltd, 1969
Historic Railway Disasters, O. S. Nock, fourth edition revised by B. K. Cooper, Ian Allan, 1987
A Pictorial Record of Southern Signals, G. Pryer, OPC, 1977
Red for Danger, L. T. C. Rolt, revised edition, Pan Books, 1966
The Victorian Railway & how it evolved, P.J.G. Ransom, Heinemann, 1990
A Guide to Mechanical Locking Frames, Signalling Study Group, 1989
The Signalbox, Signalling Study Group, OPC, 1986
Safe Railway Working, Clement E. Stretton, Crosby Lockwood, 1887
Tyer's Block Telegraph and Electric Locking Signals, Fifth Edition, Tyer, 1874
Tyer & Company Ltd, Electrical & Mechanical Signalling Engineers, Tyer trade catalogue, 1923 edition with additions
A Pictorial Record of Great Western Signalling, A. Vaughan, OPC, 1973
Exeter West Box, A. Vaughan, Exeter West Group, 1984
A Pictorial Record of LMS Signals, L. G Warburton & V. R. Anderson, OPC, 1972
Mechanical Railway Signalling, H. Rayner Wilson, 1904 (photocopy, Peter Kay, 1994)
Power Railway Signalling, H. Rayner Wilson, 1908

Railway signalling, no matter how sophisticated, is a means of communication between a moving train and stationary operating staff. Basically this communication 1) tells a driver when to start and stop, (either in the normal course of events or because of emergencies), helps regulate the speed of a train when in motion, and 2) tells him where he is going when there are alternative routes available, (junctions, sidings, platforms, etc). Obviously these two categories are not mutually exclusive, and both involve anticipation, the most important reason for providing communication between track and train.

In the early days of railway travel when horses were still being used on colliery lines, low speeds meant that controlling the passage of a train along a line was well within the capabilities of the man leading the horse. The driver's normal human reaction time to what he saw, was usually sufficient to control his train safely. Where the train was going could also be easily determined by looking to see which way points were set. With the advent of a new generation of standard gauge, passenger-carrying, main lines, beginning with the Liverpool & Manchester Railway in 1830, attitudes to operating trains had to change. A fast horse-drawn mail coach could avoid obstacles; a speeding train could not. Manoeuvres on a railway had to be anticipated and communicated to train drivers in advance.

There were two basic developments which aided this anticipation and communication:

1) the evolution of mechanical 'fixed signals' and the mechanisms to work them, and 2) the perfecting of the electric telegraph. In the first two decades following the opening of the L&MR, progress was made in both these areas, but the resulting developments were seldom combined. The advantages of using mechanical and electrical devices together were obvious to those who developed the electric telegraph, but it was not until the 1860s that mechanical and electrical equipment was installed under one roof in signalboxes whose specific function was the control not only of train movements within the limits of stations, but also along the stretches of line between stations and signalboxes. Once that principal had been established, the fundamentals of railway signalling altered very little for the next 100 years.

Below:
The signalman at Bentley prepares to catch the hoop and pouch containing the Tyer's tablet for the Bordon branch from the fireman. *E. C. Griffith.*

Following page:
A BR (WR) route indicator beneath a standard GWR/BR (WR) lower quadrant semaphore at Worcester Shrub Hill informing the driver the route is set for the Hereford line through Foregate Street station. *J. Checkley*

THE FIXED SIGNAL

When the Liverpool & Manchester Railway opened in September 1830, it is said that railway policemen were positioned along the line approximately every mile. Their job was to prevent trespass and damage, and perhaps to reassure those early railway travellers by their presence. They were also expected to communicate the state of the line to passing drivers by various gestures. For example, standing erect with arms outstretched was a signal that the line was free of obstruction, ie 'all clear.' (On other lines this became a 'danger' signal.) In reality, this must have been of marginal benefit to footplate crews who would still have had to look out very carefully to see these policemen and their gestures, and having seen them, might still have had the same time to react to a signal to stop as if they had spotted danger themselves.

Fortunately, although steam technology was still new and therefore prone to breakdowns requiring the help of lineside policemen, (arrival times of trains on the L&MR were not guaranteed for many years), there were only five daily passenger train departures from both Liverpool and Manchester when that line opened, and consequently there was little chance of collisions by one train overrunning another. The vigilance and natural range of drivers' eyesight supplemented by gesticulating policemen was sufficient for safe operation.

By the end of the 1830s, however, the number of passenger trains on the L&MR had doubled, and there were always additional specials as well as goods trains to contend with. At stations, the men operating points — 'pointsmen' — could usually see all the trains under their control, but because there was no communication between stations, once a train was out of sight, its progress could not be monitored. The company's timetable could not always be maintained, but an interval of time was still the only way of controlling trains travelling between stations on the same line. If a train had only just passed him, a policeman would stop a following train by facing it with his arms held aloft, and/or by showing a red flag or lamp at night, ('danger'). Once a specific period of time had elapsed as set down in the rule book, a 'caution' signal could be given by 'standing easy' and holding out a green flag or lamp. After another interval of time when it was assumed that the train had travelled sufficiently far ahead of any

following train, the 'all clear' signal could be given by standing to attention and/or with a white flag or lamp. Once this signal had been given, the line was assumed to be clear until the next train passed by.

Flags held little higher than the height of the average man, however, must have been difficult to see, so to improve visibility, some flags were hoisted on posts. Needless to say, it was not long before more substantial indications became necessary and these began to take the form of various shaped and painted boards — 'fixed signals'. Boards with semi-circular tops were used on the Grand Junction Railway when it opened in 1837. If the board was visible, ie face on to the approaching train, this was a signal to stop, and if it was invisible, ie edge on, this was to be taken as an 'all clear' signal. Like hand signals, boards indicating 'danger' were only displayed for a set time after the passage of a train, and at all other times were kept in the 'all clear' position.

Fixed signals seem to have been used first at junctions, as they were (and still are) more dangerous places than stations and open track. At Corbett's Lane Junction between the London & Croydon and London & Greenwich Railways, a circular board was erected when the former opened in 1839. If the points were set for the Croydon line the full face of the board was displayed, supplemented at night by a red light. If the board was edge on, or showing a white light, the points were set for the Greenwich line. This arrangement, of course, only told the driver which route was set, not whether it was safe to proceed or not. At Newton (Warrington) Junction on the L&MR, that company's first 'fixed signals' consisted of three boards painted with a chequered pattern of red and white, erected on posts 12ft high to protect trains approaching from Liverpool, Warrington and Manchester. If the boards could be seen by the drivers, then they had to be prepared to stop, and if the boards could not be seen (ie were edge on), then the line ahead of them was assumed to be clear.

Gradually a certain standard grew up in the use of fixed signals, but there were still a variety of interpretations. For example, on the Edinburgh & Glasgow Railway, two-position boards and coloured flags were used in a creative and interesting way. In the Company's Rules & Regulations book of January 1842, the following procedure was to be employed if a stations' 'Signal Porter', not wanting to exhibit a red 'danger' signal and consequently stop a train, merely wanted to pass on a 'guidance' message to a driver:

'...the Signal Porter shall, besides presenting the Green side of the fixed Signal, wave up and down his Green hand-Signal; on observing which, the Engineman shall come to such a slow motion as will enable the Porter to run alongside of the Engine, and communicate ... to the Engineman.'

At junctions and terminal stations the two indications possible using rotating boards was appropriate for the operating practices at such locations, but on stretches of line operated on the 'time-interval' system, three indications were required. Most railways had adopted this system by the end of the 1830s, and in January 1841 at a meeting of a number of companies, it was agreed that the colours used by the L&MR to indicate 'danger' (red), 'caution' (green) and 'all clear' (white) should become the standard.

Not surprisingly then, that same year witnessed the installation of one of the first fixed signals capable of showing three indications. At New Cross Gate on the L&CR, a signal was erected consisting of a narrow board, or more accurately an 'arm', pivoted at right angles to its post — the first 'semaphore' to be used for railway signalling. In some popular railway histories, the company's engineer, C. H. Gregory is credited with inventing this piece of equipment. However, it must be remembered that similar semaphores had been used as mechanical telegraphs since 1815, and would have been familiar to anyone living within sight of the Admiralty Semaphore Telegraph lines between London and Dover, and London, Portsmouth and the south coast of England, as well as to people along the line of the Holyhead–Liverpool telegraph in the late 1820s. Interestingly, by 1846, the Eastern Counties Railway was mounting non-operating telegraph semaphore arms on some of its posts carrying electric telegraph wires, to indicate to drivers how far away from stations they were.

As with the board signals, the new railway semaphore signals indicated 'danger' by facing the approaching train, (horizontal at 90° to the post) and 'all clear' by being out of sight, in this case by disappearing into a slot in the post. 'Caution' was indicated by the semaphore arm inclined down at 45°. On double track it was usual to place the arms controlling both lines into the same slot in the post, and in this double-armed form, the fixed semaphore signal quickly became a standard installation at passenger stations, contractors such as Stevens & Son of Southwark able to

supply and install them to order. *(See photo 1)*

The semaphore signal did not, however, completely supplant other types of board signals for many years, and some of these and their posts became very ornate and decorative. The London & North Western Railway, the oldest section of which included the L&MR, continued to use board signals alongside newer semaphore signals until the early 1860s. The Great Western Railway, which had inherited from its first engineer, I. K. Brunel, an individualistic approach to all aspects of mechanical engineering, made no use of semaphores until 1865.

That company's first fixed signals consisted of a ball with lamp attached which when hoisted to the top of a post signified 'all clear', and when at the bottom, 'danger'. Like Gregory's semaphore, this mechanism also had a precedent, in this case a ball mounted on top of a 15ft mast on the Octagon Room of the Greenwich Observatory in 1833. The normal position of the ball was at the top of the post (as it was with the GWR's signal), but at one o'clock it dropped to the bottom of the mast to give sailors on the Thames a precise indication of time.

A little later the GWR produced an equally individualistic three-position signal in the form of a semi-circular frame onto which could be unfurled either a red or green canvas, the 'all clear' signal being indicated when no canvases were visible. However, when the company installed fixed signals along its main line in 1843, the equipment was far more practical and in one very important respect far superior to anything then in use. On other railways, the absence of an indication on a fixed signal was taken as the 'all clear', a potentially very dangerous assumption, but with the GWR's new signals, 'all clear' and 'danger' were both positive indications.

Painted boards were mounted on the top of very tall posts, some 60ft high and the 'all clear' signal was indicated by a red circular board displayed face on to approaching trains. The 'danger' indication was given when the disc was turned edge on to traffic revealing a red cross-bar a little lower down the post. Unfortunately, although the 'all clear' was a positive indication, it was completely opposite to the meaning given to similar red boards so displayed by the majority of other

Opposite (1):

The double-armed station semaphore signal at Tunbridge Wells as drawn and lithographed by John Cooke Bourne in the 1840s. *Ironbridge Gorge Museum Trust; Elton Collection*

railway companies who used red discs face on to signify 'danger'.

Later refinements to the GWR's 'disc and cross-bar' signals included the addition of 'tails' pointing downwards to those cross-bars controlling down lines, to distinguish them from plain bars which controlled up lines. 'Tails' pointing both up and down were added to signals controlling both lines at level crossings.

Because the signals only gave two indications, 'caution' was originally made by turning an additional arrow-shaped or fishtailed board, at the foot of the post, away from the line so that its green side faced approaching trains. The board's other side, painted red, when pointed towards the line, meant 'danger'. 'All clear' was another negative signal with the board turned edge on to make it invisible to drivers. *(See photo 2)* Eventually a revolving lamp capable of projecting a red, green or white light was added to turn the 'disc & crossbar' signal into a three-position one.

THE DISTANT SIGNAL

No matter how crude or sophisticated these early fixed signals were, however, they were only of use if a driver had sufficient time to react to their indications, particularly 'danger' ones. The seriousness of a 'danger' signal could vary and depended on the reasons for the signal being exhibited. If 'danger' was displayed because a preceding train had just passed by and was running away from the fixed signal, then there was far less 'danger' than if a train was actually standing near the fixed signal waiting for the line ahead to become clear. In the latter case the fixed signal offered virtually no protection for the stationary train if another was approaching from behind.

As early as 1832 following a rear-end collision on the L&MR, policemen or gatemen were obliged to protect such stationary trains in fog by going back 300yd with their flags. (This was later increased to 400yd, a protection distance that remained standard to the end of steam on British railways.) During the 1840s as the speed that locomotives could attain increased but braking power remained crude, it became even more imperative that drivers should be able to anticipate the indications of fixed signals. By

then, going back along the line to protect a train detained by a fixed signal at 'danger' had become standard practice, and as well as taking a flag with him, the guard was expected to place detonators on the line at intervals behind the train. Detonators or 'exploding signals' had been developed in 1841 by E. A. Cowper and were adopted by the L&MR, for example, in 1844.

To protect a stationary train at a fixed signal without the need for a guard or policeman to walk back, the obvious answer was to erect another fixed signal some distance away from, (or to use later railway terminology, 'in rear of') the main station or junction board/semaphore in order to repeat the indication of the latter. Where this additional fixed signal was erected, it soon became known as the 'auxiliary', or 'distant' signal, and on most railways it was connected to a wire, or wires, and operated from a lever near the main fixed signal. An early Midland Railway Rules & Regulations book actually differentiated between 'Semaphore Signals' and 'Wire Signals', the latter being boards.

The new signal's function of giving advanced warning to drivers, however, was interpreted by different companies in two slightly different ways. To illustrate these differences, we need only look at the Rules & Regulations books of the Eastern Counties and Great Northern Railways of the mid-1850s. On the former 'auxiliary' signals were placed about 600yd in rear of the main semaphore post, and apart from 'caution' which was not shown, the 'auxiliary' repeated the indications of the main semaphore. The usual indication was 'all clear', and after a train had passed by, it was placed at 'danger'. Rule No 38 and 78 then stated that,

'Should a train arrive before the Line is clear, it must be brought to a stand outside the Auxiliary Post, after which the Signal must be lowered to allow the Train to pass within its protection, and then be placed again at Danger and remain so whilst the Train is at, and until it has got clear away from the Station.'

This method of working made the 'auxiliaries' more like extra stop signals. In later railway parlance, if the main fixed signal is considered to be the 'starter', then the 'auxiliary' becomes the 'home' signal, or if the main fixed signal is considered the 'home' signal, then the 'auxiliary' becomes an 'outer home.'

When A. Sturrock the GNR's Locomotive Superintendent suggested in 1851 that 'distant' signals should be erected 1,000yd or 1,200yd in rear of the main fixed signals where they were out of sight on curves, or on gradients of 1 in 200 or more, to allow trains adequate braking distance, it appears he too expected his drivers to be able to stop at those signals. By the mid-1850s, however, the signals had obviously taken on a more 'cautionary' role, very like that of distants in later 'block working.' In the company's Rules & Regulations of April 1855, if a driver saw a distant at 'danger', he had to control his locomotive so as to be able to stop at that signal, but if on seeing all was clear, was empowered to pass it at 5mph.

THE LEVER FRAME & INTERLOCKING

During the 1840s, all the fixed signals described above, whether semaphores or boards, would have been operated from handles attached to the posts on which the signals were mounted, or from levers close by, and in the case of 'distant' signals, from simple levers attached to them by iron wires. The safe operation of these fixed signals, along with points at junctions and for sidings, was entirely dependent on the particular operator (policeman, pointsman, signal porter, etc) abiding by the companies' rules and regulations. Inevitably, there were occasions when signals were incorrectly operated, a particularly hazardous possibility if the indications of signals at junctions did not reflect the position of the points.

As with the development of fixed signals, junctions, being some of the most dangerous locations on railways, remained the focus for signalling innovations, and to clarify what follows, it should be noted that by the 1840s, junction semaphores generally gave only two indications — horizontal for danger and inclined downwards at 45° for 'proceed' (cautiously) — the normal position of the arms being 'danger' until a train was required to pass over the points.

The first example of a mechanical device to prevent conflicting signal indications being displayed at such locations was installed at the simple double line Bricklayers Arms Junction on the L&CR in 1843/4. The device, to the designs of C. H. Gregory, consisted of an iron frame containing four 'stirrups', each when pressed down by the signalman's foot, operating one of the two double-arm semaphores — one post carrying the two main line signals, and the other the pair of branch line ones. *(See photo 3)* When the main line signal was lowered, the stirrup which worked it pushed over a linkage

Below (3):
A pair of double-armed semaphores on a signalling platform. *Illustrated in F. S. Williams, Our Iron Roads, 1852*

JUNCTION SIGNALS.

preventing the conflicting branch line stirrup from being depressed, and vice versa.

The device was a significant development, but the mechanism was not connected in any way with the point levers, which consequently could still be worked independently of the signals to give conflicting indications. But despite its limitations, Gregory's 'stirrup' frame became the first such device to go into limited production for any railway company that wanted to buy it, manufactured by the signalling contractors Stevens & Son of Southwark.

The next logical development was to physically link the mechanisms operating points and signals, but surprisingly this did not happen for another 12 years. When a new device to achieve this did appear in 1856 (Patent No 1479) to the designs of John Saxby, a foreman at the London, Brighton & South Coast Railway's Brighton Works, it used levers to work both signals and points simultaneously. The inspiration for this mechanism is popularly believed to have stemmed from Saxby witnessing a SER train taking the wrong route at Bricklayers Arms Junction, even though the signalman there had lowered his semaphore to indicate that the points were set for the correct line. The perfection of the 'Simultaneous Motion' frame put Saxby in the forefront of signalling developments, and in 1857/8, with the blessing of his employers and the financial support of the Superintendent of the LBSCR's Goods Department, he began to manufacture his new apparatus, (although few, if any, other railway companies appeared interested).

Although two special levers were built into the 'Simultaneous Motion' frame to enable the main-line signals to be placed at 'danger' irrespective of the way the points were set, and set-screws could be used on the branch line signals to hold them at danger as well, the frame had very obvious limitations as the fundamental principle behind it was that each point had to be connected to its own signal.

Despite this shortcoming, the apparatus was championed by the Board of Trade and, in 1858, undoubtedly because it knew that Saxby could produce the appropriate equipment, its first published 'requirements' stated that at all junctions, the signals and points should be worked in 'conjunction'. The Board had no powers to force railway companies to install new equipment on existing lines, but it could prevent the opening of newly-constructed routes to passengers if it felt they were not up to standard. This the Board did at the end of 1859 when a Stevens Stirrup frame at Kentish Town Junction on the North London Railway was rejected as unsatisfactory. Not wanting to have to

purchase equipment from Saxby, the Company's Engineer, Austen Chambers, then set about modifying the existing frame to incorporate the point levers. To these he attached plates which prevented the signal stirrups from being moved if the point levers were not correctly set. When the points were in the correct position, and whilst the appropriate stirrup was depressed, the plates also 'locked' the point lever and consequently the points themselves. To apply the term 'locking' to Chamber's plates was entirely appropriate as the actual padlocking of points to prevent movement had been practised on lines such as the Edinburgh & Glasgow Railway as early as 1842.

But of more importance than the evolution of later terminology was the principle embodied in this hybrid frame that the signalman, to operate safely and achieve the desired signal indications, and because of the 'interlocking', had to move the levers and stirrups in a certain order, in a sequence of movements each interdependent, by 'successive motion'. This became the underlying principle behind all railway signalling, and is still true today. Each operation has to be carried out correctly before another can take place.

Both Stevens and Saxby realised the importance of this immediately, and by March 1860 a frame consisting of a row of fully interlocked levers operating both points and signals had been manufactured by the former and installed at Yeovil Junction. Four months later, Saxby patented his own version of the interlocking lever frame, and as was to become typical of the man and his business, promptly took Stevens to court claiming infringement of his new patent!

THE SIGNALBOX
The fundamental principle of 'interlocking' embodied in these new frames, came just a few years before most railway companies were prepared to invest seriously in what were fairly complex pieces of machinery. Nevertheless, during the 1850s as station layouts had become more complex, and trains more frequent, the traditional method of working signals and points largely independently, was tending towards the employment of many more operating staff. Therefore, as well as the Board of Trade's desire for greater safety, there was a financial incentive to develop more efficient operating practices, by bringing the levers that worked points and signals physically closer together so that they could be controlled by fewer men. By the end of the decade, this form of 'concentration' was one of the Board of Trade's strongest

recommendations.

At the same time, signal 'towers' and 'platforms' had begun to appear, to give 'signalmen', (this term by then having largely superseded railway 'policemen'), a better view of the area under their supervision. *(See photo 4)*

Although these structures did not originally include the equipment for working all points and signals under a signalman's control, they were the obvious structures in which to concentrate such apparatus and this is just what the Board of Trade began to push for in the late 1850s.

The signalling 'platform' apart from a small hut for the signalman, tended to be, as the term implies, open to the elements, with the semaphores or boards and the equipment for operating them, outside on the timber staging. When Saxby developed his 'Simultaneous Motion' equipment, however, the platform on which it was mounted was completely protected by timber and glazed walls and a pitched roof, forming in effect a complete cabin from which the semaphores then rose out of the roof. (Whether intentional or not, this arrangement closely resembled the earlier generation of mechanical telegraph stations which also consisted of a small single operating room with semaphores, or shutters, above.)

Between 1857 and 1862, the LB&SCR, for which Saxby still worked, erected a number of these distinctive elevated 'cabins', which soon proved ideal structures into which Saxby's new, mechanically more complicated and longer interlocking lever frames could be fitted, as well as the necessary electrical equipment for operating the 'block' system (see below) introduced between London and Brighton at the end of 1862.

Saxby's elevated cabins and the equipment they contained, immediately became the standard by which all subsequent 'signalboxes' were measured, and with the benefit of hindsight, they were obviously used by other railway companies and signalling contractors as models for many later structures.

Below (4):
Clayton Tunnel on the London, Brighton & South Coast Railway in the mid-1860s showing the very meagre signalling platform and hut. This would have contained the telegraph instruments as the tunnel was controlled by 'Absolute Block Working' before the rest of the main line. *Lens of Sutton*

The development of the electric telegraph coincided exactly with the first phase of major railway building following on from the success of the Liverpool & Manchester Railway. Yet as a means of safely controlling the passage of trains between stations, it was not generally taken up by railway companies until the 1860s. Apart from handling general messages, its only application to railway signalling until then was the regulating of trains through tunnels, and even then it was not always thought to be 100% reliable by some railway managers.

The new main line railways of the 1830s and 1840s were built by men more familiar with, and certain of, the robust products of civil engineering and solid blacksmithing, than the delicate art of electrical and instrument engineering. Until the 1860s, the running and control of trains was predominantly a mechanical exercise. From the steam locomotives to the timber fixed signals and iron levers, it was genuinely believed that safety could be attained by the employment of alert and physically strong men, adhering strictly to the companies' rules and regulations. The electric telegraph was seen by many railway companies as little more than an interesting supplement to the necessary physical human skills of railway operation. From the first experiments in the late 1830s it took over 20 years before the telegraph was considered reliable enough to be essential for safe railway operation.

The result of the first electric telegraph patent of June 1837 was an elegant instrument which has become probably one of the most familiar objects in the history of electricity. The diamond-shaped instrument constructed to the designs of W. F. Cooke and Charles Wheatstone was the first to use centrally pivoted vertical needles, (four or five in the initial design), which could be deflected either to the right or left depending on the direction of the current. All subsequent telegraph instruments, and those block instruments which evolved from them to become the most widely-employed form of electrical signalling device, made use of the centrally-pivoted vertical needle.

Having unsuccessfully tried to persuade the L&MR to install an electric telegraph circuit between Edge Hill and Lime Street, Cooke approached the chairman of the London & Birmingham Railway just as that line was nearing completion in the summer of 1837. Although Robert Stephenson was obviously fascinated by the demonstration that Cooke set up with his support in July that year, and was impressed by the experimental telegraph operated between Euston and Camden Town at the end of the month, the directors of the L&BR decided not to adopt the system.

Fortunately a more fruitful liaison developed only two months later when Cooke was approached by I. K. Brunel, and by April 1838 he had persuaded the Great Western Railway to agree to let Cooke install the electric telegraph between Paddington and West Drayton at the Company's expense. A year later five-needle instruments, connected by six wires, had been installed between Paddington and Hanwell, an additional circuit being run to West Drayton by July 1839. To test the system, the time that every train passed West Drayton and Hanwell was successfully telegraphed to Paddington for a period of two months. From then on the system was only used to send and receive general information and was not used in any real sense to control the passage of trains between stations. Although the telegraph was eventually extended to Slough in 1843, a link which attracted considerable public attention in 1845 when it was used to inform the police in London of the flight of murderer John Tawell from that town, who as a result was arrested when his train arrived at Paddington, the telegraph was taken out of use in 1849.

The installation had never been intended to regulate train movements, of course, and as far as this function was concerned, the electric telegraph's potential was first demonstrated on the London & Blackwall Railway which opened as a self-contained line between Blackwall and Minories in 1840, being extended to Fenchurch Street in 1841. Robert Stephenson as one of its engineers, was obviously instrumental in getting Cooke & Wheatstone's electric telegraph installed. The line was worked by reciprocating cable haulage and carriages were attached to, and/or detached from, this cable at the closely spaced intermediate stations. Each station had a single-needle telegraph instrument, on which the centrally pivoted vertical needle could be deflected one way to indicate 'ready', and the opposite way to indicate 'stop'. At the terminal stations all the intermediate station's indications were repeated on a combined instrument. An electrical bell was used to 'call attention' of the winding drum brakesmen and enginemen, and by deflecting the needle to the appropriate indication, the appropriate action could be taken.

In the light of how needle instruments were used in later 'block working', it was significant that each single-needle in the Blackwall system pointed directly to a full message, unlike in the GWR system where a number of needles deflecting in relation to each other had to be read in sequence to build up a complete message. The way in which the GWR instruments were used made them the direct precursors of the 'speaking telegraph' instruments, usually containing just one or sometimes two needles which were deflected from side to side to spell out a message (eventually using the Morse Code [left — dot, right — dash]). The way in which the Blackwall instruments were used made them the direct ancestors of 'block telegraph' instruments, *(see Chapter 3)*.

Following the success of the Blackwall system, Cooke published a book entitled *Telegraphic Railways* in 1842, which outlined the advantages of using the electric telegraph on single lines. Taking a stretch of the new Midland Counties Railway as a theoretical example, he divided the line up into 'Grand Divisions' of between 15 and 25 miles long with a principal station at either end, each 'Division' further subdivided into 'Stages' of between two and five miles long. Every 'Stage' had a telegraph instrument capable of showing the indications of every other 'Stage,' whilst at the principal stations at either end of the 'Grand Division', instruments there showed the indications of all the intermediate instruments. The normal position of each needle was upright, and when inclined to the left or right indicated whether a train was approaching in the 'up' or 'down' direction. Obviously when the needle showed that a train was travelling in the 'up' direction, a railway policeman knew he could not send a train in the 'down' direction.

As Cooke's system could also increase the capacity and efficient running of single lines it is not surprising that the single-needle telegraph was soon in use on such railways. One of the first companies to use the electric telegraph to regulate trains, was the Norwich & Yarmouth Railway opened in April 1844. Once again Robert Stephenson was the engineer. Four months later, the single line of the South Eastern Railway between Tonbridge and Maidstone opened, also equipped with Cooke & Wheatstone's single-needle instruments.

Following on from its obviously successful application to single lines, the electric telegraph was not immediately taken up on double-line railways apart from regulating the passage of trains through tunnels. The use of the electric telegraph through Clay Cross Tunnel on the North Midland Railway as early as 1840, is now disputed, as is the claim that Clayton Tunnel on the London, Brighton & South Coast Railway was so equipped in 1841, *(See Photo 4)* but there is no doubt that both tunnels were eventually protected in this way by the 1850s. A more reliable date can be given for the installation of the electric telegraph through Box Tunnel on the Great Western Railway — 1847.

One feature of Cooke & Wheatstone's first electric telegraphs which made them expensive to install and maintain was the requirement that to complete a circuit between each needle unit two line wires were needed. For multiple-needle installations, the number of wires obviously increased again, and if a system was to be installed where all the intermediate instruments' indications were to be repeated in combined instruments at the terminal stations as advocated by Cooke, then the number of wires required became considerable. A significant contribution, therefore, to the extensive use of the electric telegraph, was the discovery that the earth itself could be used as one part of a circuit — the 'earth return'.

Consequently, during the 1840s the posts and wires of the electric telegraph spread very rapidly along the routes of the country's railways, not for the control of trains, but for the transmission of messages. By 1846 there were 1,048 miles of telegraph operating throughout the country. By the beginning of the next decade, the South Eastern Railway was particularly well-equipped with both single and double-needle telegraph instruments, but although its system probably had more to do with the running of trains than most, it was used to monitor rather than control the movement of trains so that decisions could be made about shunting them out of the way at intermediate stations, or summoning assisting engines, or advising stations of the running of special trains. Public messages were also dealt with over the same system. Signalmen still had no direct link with the telegraph, and continued to dispatch trains according to the timetable and 'time interval' working.

By the mid-1850s the 'time interval' system was barely coping with the increasing number of trains running on an expanding network of lines throughout the country. The most significant increase was in goods traffic, and particularly in the transport of coal from the North and Midlands to London. In 1841 receipts from freight totalled £866,000, less than a third of the amount generated from passenger traffic. By 1861 the figure had risen to £14,699,000, and exceeded passenger receipts by quite a margin. The railways and the coal trade were becoming inextricably linked, and companies like the Midland, North Eastern, Great Northern, Manchester, Sheffield & Lincolnshire, and London & North Western Railways, were all contributing to the rapid expansion of the country's coalfields.

As the number of trains increased, so too did their speeds. The problem was not the speeds themselves, however, but the increasing differences between them. Whereas goods trains continued to rumble up and down the country at virtually the same rate as a decade before, the speed of passenger trains improved noticeably. For example, in 1842 it could take a passenger 6hr to reach Nottingham from London, whereas in 1862 it was possible to do the journey in 3hr. So although goods were more remunerative than passenger trains, they became a growing problem operationally. The ultimate solution for the major companies was to lay separate and largely independent lines for their slower-moving freight trains, but in the 1850s double track had to suffice, and consequently running trains by the 'time interval' system was becoming potentially more dangerous than it had been a decade before.

By the mid-1850s many Rules & Regulations books were instructing signalmen to allow only 5min gaps between 'danger', 'caution' and 'all clear' indications on their fixed signals. There was little margin for error. Some railways coped by positioning signalmen within sight of each other, as on the East Lancashire Railway, but this was certainly not practicable on all lines. Significantly, on the Great Northern Railway, which having completed its main line in 1852 was running some of the fastest passenger trains anywhere in the country, the Rules & Regulations book of April 1855, revised 1867, instructed signalmen to display the 'caution' indication on their fixed signals for 13min after 'danger' had been exhibited for 5min. The

company clearly appreciated the risks of fast running and poor braking.

The dangers were all too obvious, and what was essential to improve safety was that the aspects of the fixed signals should indicate the actual, and not the presumed state of the line ahead.

In this decade, therefore, Cooke's theories were examined again, and within a few years, three crucial elements in the creation of an effective system which could be used to separate trains by space and not time — the 'Block System' — were put into operation.

The first element, which actually gave rise to the term 'block system', was the dividing up of railways into sections or blocks, controlled at either end by signalmen operating fixed signals. These were the equivalent of Cooke's 'stages'. On railways like the SE, where passenger stations and junctions were comparatively close together, the stretches of line between stations and junctions logically became the first block sections. On other routes where the distances between stations and junctions were longer, it was inevitable that purpose-built intermediate 'signal stations' would have to be provided if the sections were not to reduce the capacity of the line. Resistance to this financial commitment delayed the introduction of block working on many lines.

The second element was the use of appropriate electrical equipment to enable signalmen to communicate with each other, so that they knew when and what sort of train had been dispatched into the block section, and whether it had arrived safely at the other end. Here the electric telegraph finally came into its own.

The third, and crucial, element in the successful implementation of the new system, demanded that both the electrical equipment and the fixed signals should be under the direct control of signalmen at either end of each block section.

THE FIRST BLOCK BELLS

The first electrical equipment to be used purely for block working was the single-stroke bell. In 1851, Charles V. Walker, Telegraph Superintendent of the SER, had such bells installed on that company's lines so that signalmen could communicate the passage of trains between stations by the sending and receiving of coded messages made up of a certain number and combination of beats on the bell. By this method, the SER became the first to operate block working over its entire main line. When Walker's bells were introduced, point and signal levers were still not concentrated together at every station, and therefore, signalmen were not always within earshot of their bells when messages were transmitted. So pointers were added to them to give a visual record of the number of beats sent.

THE FIRST BLOCK INSTRUMENTS

The man responsible for advocating dividing up a railway into sections other than those between passenger stations, involving the erection of signal stations, and the employment of special telegraph instruments exclusively for indicating whether the line was clear for the passage of trains or not, was Edwin Clark, Chief Engineer of the Electric Telegraph Company, (the firm set up in 1845 by W. F. Cooke, after his partnership with Charles Wheatstone had broken down).

The first railway company to adopt his system was the London & North Western Railway. The impetus for its installation was a need to increase line capacity without having to lay additional tracks. In 1846 the pressure to do this had been resisted on the route between London and Rugby by installing the electric telegraph, which like that on the SER was used to monitor the progress of trains between stations more effectively so that

decisions could be made about shunting slow-moving ones out of the way for others to pass by. But between 1846 and 1853 the number of trains running on this stretch of railway had increased by 48%, and therefore the alternatives were once again to either lay separate goods lines, or to make more effective use of the telegraph system for the control of trains. Because the latter was the cheapest, it became the preferred option and installation work began in 1855.

Between London and Rugby the railway was divided up into block sections each approximately two miles long. At each end of these sections where there was not already a passenger station or junction platform with fixed signals, simple brick towers were erected around which elevated timber platforms were constructed about 10ft off the ground. The signalman in each tower controlled a number of fixed signals (not always physically operated from the tower), and inside the single room, two telegraph instruments were installed each with two separate centrally pivoted vertical needles, one for the 'up' line and one for the 'down'. Each instrument had two handles which when moved to the right or left activated the electrical circuit for each needle. By pointing the needle to one side 'line clear' could be indicated, and to the other 'train on line'. Normally the handles were held over to the left thereby allowing current to continue to flow through the coils maintaining the needles at 'line clear'. When trains passed between the signal stations, the handles at both stations were moved to the right so that the needle indicated 'train on line'. Metal pegs attached to the instruments by short chains were used to keep the handles in the appropriate position, giving rise to the term 'pegging instrument', or in signalman's slang, 'pegger'. *(See photo 5)* If a train ran into trouble out of sight of a signal station, train crews were instructed to cut through the telegraph wires which of course meant that the instrument needles dropped by gravity to an intermediate position between 'line clear' and 'train on line' — 'line blocked'.

Unlike in Cooke's Blackwall or Norfolk Railway systems, the route between London and Rugby did not constitute a 'Grand Division', with all the signal stations instrument indications repeated on master instruments at either end. In the LNWR

Left (5):
The peg and chain arrangement used on the first single-needle block instruments.
National Railway Museum Collection

system there were complete and independent circuits between each tower, the relevant deflections of the needles only being sent and received at adjacent signal stations. As well as being a significant break with telegraph practice, this arrangement obviously reduced installation costs, and was probably more reliable in operation.

Within a few years, electric bells were added to the system so that the signalmen's attention could be attracted audibly when indications on the instruments were about to be altered, and in this form the LNWR's system was a major advance in train control. But it also had a major weakness. The principal safety feature made possible by the block system, ie the permitting of only one train at a time into a block section, was not adopted. Because the LNWR believed this would cause delays, signalmen were allowed to send more than one train travelling in the same direction into the section between signal stations. The needles remained at 'Train on Line' no matter how many trains passed through the section, and the signalmen had to be very careful to remember exactly which of a number of trains had arrived safely.

BLOCK INSTRUMENT EVOLUTION

Despite this the LNWR system undoubtedly laid the foundations for 'traditional' signalling practice, and the significance was not lost on other contemporary railway managers, and particularly on the inventive Victorian electrical engineers' minds. This observation is borne out by the fact that during the 1860s all but a few of the electrical instruments that were destined to control the block system for over a century, were developed and put into use for the first time.

The first generation of these purpose-designed 'block instruments' fall into two categories:

1) those which indicated the state of the line, and

2) those which effectively told a signalman what indications his fixed signals should display.

Those in the first category were direct descendants of electric telegraph instruments and ultimately better suited to controlling the block system than those in the second category, which although surviving in a few areas until the 1980s, were conceptually redundant by the 1880s.

CATEGORY ONE

i) Tyer's one-wire, two-position block instruments.

Edward Tyer took out his first patent for a signalling device at the start of 1852, and in concept it was far ahead of its time. Perhaps because of this it was not widely adopted, but undeterred, Tyer continued to develop and patent other unique devices for train signalling during the next 10 years. Eventually it was his simple-to-install and cost-effective block instruments which could be straightforwardly manipulated by signalmen that established his company as the most important manufacturer of electrical signalling equipment in the world.

In 1862, he was granted a patent, (No 3015) for a block instrument obviously based on Clark's work, but with all the four needles required for controlling a double line either side of a signal station, incorporated into one case. Instead of handles to operate the needles, the instrument had brass plungers, and in this form it was exhibited in London at the International Exhibition of that year. (See photo 6) Some railway managers probably felt it was too confusing for ordinary signalman to understand, but there were two powerful selling points, which when incorporated into later Tyer's instruments finally convinced many Board of Directors to purchase:

1) only one wire was needed to connect instruments at either end of a block section (with the usual earth return) compared with the three wires needed to operate Clark's block instruments. Tyer's single-wire, earth return circuit, included a single-stroke bell (for signalling 'up' trains), and a single-stroke gong (for signalling 'down' trains), whereas Clark's bells and needles all required separate circuits;

2) there was a considerable saving on battery power because the instruments did not use continuous currents to maintain the needles at either 'line clear' or 'train on line'. By pressing down one of the appropriate plungers on the front of the instrument case, the circuit was activated between the 'sending' and 'receiving' instruments. The appropriate plunger rang either the bell or gong, and whilst it was depressed, the current temporarily magnetised metal pieces around the appropriate needles on both the sending and receiving instruments. When the plunger was released thereby stopping the flow of current, the metal pieces retained their magnetism, thus maintaining the needles at one of two possible indications — 'line clear' or 'train on line'. This momentary current principle was taken up by other electrical engineers to save battery power.

Over the next few years, Tyer refined the electrical mechanisms of his instrument, particularly in the area of counteracting the effects of lightning, and when Patent No 2907 was granted to him in 1869, he had all the

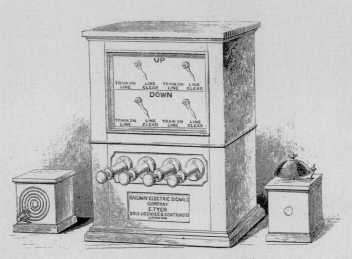

TYER'S TRAIN SIGNALLING TELEGRAPH.

elements to enable him to create what became one of the most commercially successful block instruments. Instead of putting all the needles into one case, he adopted Clark's idea of producing an instrument with two needles, so that two identical instruments would be needed for each signalbox controlling ordinary double track. A separate plunger was provided with each set so that the bell or gong could be activated without the signalman inadvertently changing the indication of the needles, and in this form, and also in a version with miniature semaphore arms substituted for the needles, Tyer's Train Signalling Telegraph instruments became popular with a number of important railway companies in the 1870s.

ii) Spagnoletti's three-wire, two-position block instrument.

Charles E. Spagnoletti had worked for the Electric Telegraph Company before moving to the Great Western Railway in 1855 at the age of 23, and therefore he would also have been aware of Edwin Clark's work on the LNWR. Not surprisingly, when he developed a block instrument for the GWR he too based his ideas around the principle of the single needle. The patent for his device was granted

on 10 February 1863 (No 2297), but instead of a vertical needle pointing to a description, as in Clark's instrument, Spagnoletti attached to the top of his needle a card (referred to in the patent as a 'screen', and later in more common usage as a 'disc') on which were printed opposite each other the words 'line clear', on a white ground, and 'train on line', on a red ground. In his block instrument the needle was then mounted behind a painted metal screen in which there was a small rectangular aperture through which one of the printed indications would show when the current was flowing in the appropriate direction. To complete the circuit so that 'line clear' showed in the aperture, the left-hand one of two 'tappers', (or 'finger keys' as stated in the patent), protruding from the front of the instrument, was held down by a metal peg. When that was released, the peg was then used to hold down the right-hand finger key, causing 'train on line' to be displayed in the aperture. The 'line clear' tapper had a white end, whilst the 'train on line' one had a red end.

As with Clark and Tyer's instruments, the normal indication was 'line clear', only changed by the signalman to 'train on line' when a train entered the block section. The signalman sending a train forward into a block section pegged down 'train on line' and when the disc of the instrument at the far end also displayed this indication, the signalman there pegged down his red finger key. When the train reached the far end of the section, the signalman there unpegged the 'train on line' indication and pegged 'line clear'. On receiving this indication, the signalman at the place from where the train had been sent,

also pegged down his white finger key. *(See photo 7)*

With the refinement of the block system in the 1870s, the pegging instrument was joined by a 'non-pegging' variation, a needle unit in an identical case, but without the finger keys. If a train was going forward into a block section, the signalman in advance pegged down 'train on line' as before, but the indication was repeated at the end the train was being sent from, on the 'non-pegging' instrument. As three separate instruments were required to control the passage of trains between adjacent signalboxes — a pegger, non-pegger, and single-stroke bell — and each of those instruments was connected by its own wire (with earth return), the terminology to describe Spagnoletti's (and others') continuous current system was 'three-wire'. (For a full description of block working see Chapter 5 Part 1.)

Of all the early block instruments, Spagnoletti's changed the least after it had been patented. The only significant

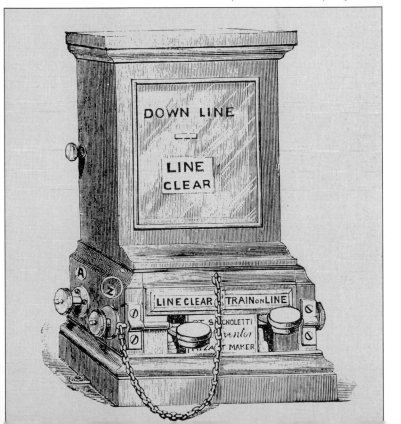

modifications in later instruments were the attaching of the descriptions to the bottom of the needle instead of the top, the replacement of the peg and chain by a loop of wire, and much later the addition of brass reminder flaps which could be dropped down over the finger keys to prevent the signalman from depressing them.

CATEGORY TWO
As will be appreciated, if the block system was implemented 'absolutely', ie only one train in a section at a time, there was no need for the controlling semaphore to be capable of showing three indications — 'danger', 'caution' and 'clear'. Consequently, where block working was adopted, it must have become usual for the station signals to display only two aspects — either danger or clear. This should be borne in mind when considering the development of 'semaphore' block instruments.

i) Preece's three-wire, two-position block instruments
The first man to develop an instrument which effectively prompted the signalman in the use of his fixed signals, was William Preece. Preece, who had become the London & South Western Railway's Superintendent of Telegraphs in 1860, had worked as Edwin Clark's assistant whilst at the Electric Telegraph Company, and therefore was completely familiar with the LNWR's block system. The LSWR's telegraph office at Southampton used both single and double-needle telegraph instruments to transmit messages, but when Preece came to devise instruments for controlling the block system, (Patent No 77, 24 June 1862) he decided they should not inform the signalman as to the state of the line, but should be concerned with the fixed signals and their indications.

To this end Preece created two physically separate, but electrically-linked, devices. The most striking was a wooden case from which protruded a tall metal post, at the top of which was a single miniature semaphore arm. The second device was another rectangular case in which a needle indicated whether the signal was 'off' (all clear), or 'on' (danger).

Signalmen communicated by single-stroke bells, and the fundamental idea was that once a train had been allowed to enter a clear block section, the signalman who was to receive the train, pressed a 'switch key' which raised the miniature semaphore arm at the end from which the train was approaching to 'danger'. This prompted the signalman there to place his fixed signal to 'danger' thus preventing another train from entering the section. Whilst the miniature semaphore arm was in the

'danger' position, the needle pointed to the word 'on' on the other instrument at the far end of the section, to confirm to the signalman there who was awaiting the train, that the miniature semaphore at the other end was displaying the correct indication. Once the train had arrived safely, the signalman put his 'switch key' to the 'off' position, (which would be indicated by the word 'off' in the other instrument), and the miniature semaphore at the end from which the train had come would disappear into its metal post — the accepted 'all clear' position — telling the signalman there that he could once again lower his outdoor semaphore.

This system was refined over the years by the substitution of the 'switch key' (which was not illustrated in the patent) by a miniature lever with a turned wooden handle, which resembled a full-sized signal lever. In the patent details of 1865 for this miniature lever, (No 2016), Preece intended it to be used in conjunction with a wheel-operated treadle. Once put to 'danger', the lever was locked in that position until the train passed over the treadle which freed it for another 'line clear' pull. Later the 'on/off' indicator gained a circular face behind which the single-stroke bell was mounted. (See photo 9) Eventually Preece's instruments were modified to work on momentary rather than continuous currents, (as with Tyer's instruments), at which time the miniature semaphore, bell and 'on/off' indications were incorporated into a single wooden case. By then 'all clear' was indicated when the miniature semaphore was inclined at 45°, and eventually the three-wire

Opposite above (8):
Charles Walker's single-stroke bells and double semaphore block instruments can be seen at the far end of this signalbox at London Bridge station in 1866. Above the sloping desk on the left are what appear to be two Tyer's 1862 instruments. In John Saxby's lever frame on the right, the semaphore signals are controlled by the short travel levers in the centre of the frame, whilst the point levers are grouped either side. *Illustrated London News, 8 September 1866, p 241*

Opposite (9):
Instruments devised and patented by William Preece in the 1860s, in Hoist Cabin, Wakefield, Lancashire & Yorkshire Railway. *Engraving from The Railway Magazine, Vol II, 1898*

version — ie the original 1862 patent — was treated in the same way with its own wooden case.

ii) Walker's one-wire, two-position block instrument.

About the same time Preece was developing his system and instruments, C. V. Walker was being persuaded to supplement the SER's block working by coded bell messages, with an instrument which gave a visual indication.

Two instruments were devised to achieve this. The main one consisted of a wooden case containing a miniature post with a double-arm semaphore — the left hand arm being red, and the right hand arm being white. Once again the idea was that the miniature semaphores should resemble the full size ones at the signalman's 'signal station'. *(See photo 8)*

Subsequent instruments had the single-stroke bell mounted on top of the case, and it was the electrical and mechanical mechanism for moving the semaphores and sounding the bell which was patented by C. V. and A. O. Walker in 1865, (No 488). The other smaller device had two plungers, one with a white end the other with a black end. Both plungers could be used to transmit bell codes, but the one with a white end lowered the miniature white semaphore in the main instrument, whilst the one with a black end raised it.

It appears that from the start, the miniature semaphores in Walker's instrument indicated 'all clear' when inclined at 45°. With the semaphores lowered like this, the instrument was in its 'normal' position. When a train was to go forward from one 'signal station' to another, the signalman would ask permission of the signalman in advance by transmitting the appropriate bell code. If the signalman in advance was able to 'accept' the train, he would reply by repeating the code on his black plunger. When the train left the station, the signalman there would send the same coded message again, and this time the signalman in advance would reply on his white plunger. This raised the miniature white semaphore in his instrument to indicate that a train was on its way, but more importantly, it also raised the miniature red semaphore in the instrument at the station where the train was leaving, in effect telling the signalman there to put his main outdoor semaphore to danger once the train had left. Both the main semaphore and the miniature semaphore then remained at danger until the train had arrived safely at the station in advance. Once this had happened, the signalman there transmitted three beats on his black plunger, thereby lowering his white semaphore as well as the red semaphore at the other other end of the circuit, signifying that the line was clear again. This system was first operated in and out of Charing Cross when that station opened in 1864.

By the end of the 1860s, all the elements that were to remain at the heart of railway signalling for the next 100 years, were in existence and fully appreciated by railway engineers, managers, and the Railway Inspectorate of the Board of Trade. Companies like the London, Brighton & South Coast and South Eastern Railways were in the forefront of technical developments, the latter along with the Bristol & Exeter, Metropolitan and North London Railways operating most of their lines strictly by the Block System. But for the rest what was needed was the commitment, the funds and the threat of legislation to bring the elements together.

THE ESSENTIAL ELEMENTS

The following is an overview of those elements on the eve of the signalling revolution', a decade that witnessed significant investment by the country's major railway companies in the latest signalling technology, both mechanical and electrical.

1. **Rules & Regulations books** — issued by all railway companies to their staff which, although not yet standardised, contained similar and largely compatible instructions. In 1867 the General Managers' Conference at which most of the country's railway companies were represented, it was agreed that where running powers were exercised, companies should adopt common rules.

2. **Lamps on trains and engines** — all companies attached lamps to the front of their engines (usually showing a white 'clear' light), and a lamp or lamps to the rear of trains to indicate which was the last vehicle (almost invariably red — 'danger'). This lamp not only warned other trains approaching from the rear, but it also indicated to signalmen that the train was complete. Before continuous automatic brakes, divided trains were not uncommon and the problems they caused could defeat any signalling system.

3. **Fixed signals** — the majority of companies already used semaphores, or were actively converting to them.
   a) The front face of semaphore arms (including 'auxiliary' or 'distant' signals) were painted red with a white or black band or white dot, the rear coloured white with a black stripe or dot.
   b) Where semaphore arms were mounted

together on the same post, each arm reading from top to bottom controlled a separate diverging line from left to right.
   c) All companies supplemented the indications of their signals with lamps displaying coloured lights at night — red for 'danger', green for 'caution' and white for 'clear'.
   d) It was generally agreed that 'auxiliary' or 'distant' signals should show the same indication as the main 'station' semaphore to which they applied.

4. **'Speaking' telegraph** — direct descendants of Cooke & Wheatstone's telegraph, these were single-needle instruments for the transmission of messages either letter by letter or in discrete codes, (eventually the Morse Code was adopted by all railway companies). *(See photo 10)* Later instruments had small pieces of brass or tin so positioned that when the single needle deflected from side to side it struck them. These 'sounders' had slightly different tones and, therefore, signalmen were able to hear the messages being transmitted without having to look at the needle.

5. **'Block' telegraph** —
   a) single-needle instruments, both continuous and momentary-current needle type, which could indicate the state of the line — 'line clear' and 'train on line'.
   b) 'semaphore block instruments' with miniature two position semaphores, (the arms either magnetised, or activated by continuous current), to prompt the signalman in the use of his outdoor signals.

6. **Single-stroke electric bells** — usually with a tapper protruding from the front of the case so that a set number of beats on the bell signifying the type of train passing between 'signal stations' could be transmitted.

7. **Interlocking** — strongly championed by the Board of Trade, the manufacture and installation of interlocked lever frames had accelerated as the 1860s progressed. At first only Saxby and Stevens had the manufacturing capacity to produce the only pair of practical mechanisms then available, but between 1866 and 1875, 54 new patents were granted for alternative designs.
Initially Saxby's 1860 Patent lever frames were confined to the London, Brighton &

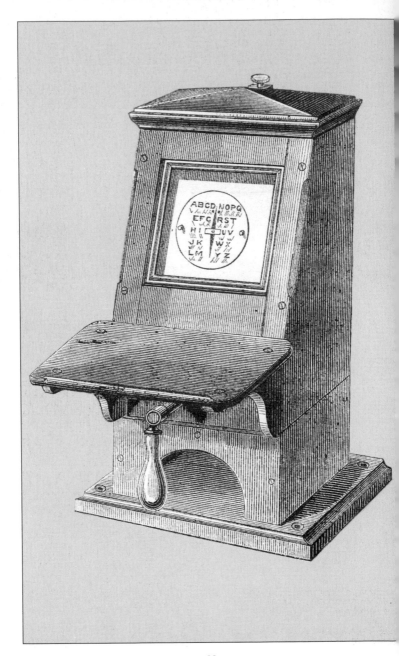

South Coast Railway, but in 1862 an agreement was signed to supply the London & North Western Railway, and by the time manufacture of this design ended in 1867, the Caledonian, Metropolitan, North Eastern and South Eastern Railways had all purchased examples.

In 1863 Saxby entered into partnership with John Farmer, and in 1867 in an attempt to design a form of locking which did not wear as badly as that in the Saxby 1860 Patent frames, the firm patented two new types of lock, 'wedge' and 'bell crank'. The latter proved more durable, and frames with this type of locking were purchased by, amongst others, the Great Eastern, Great Northern, London, Brighton & South Coast, London & North Western, London & South Western and North Eastern Railways.

Opposite (10):
Typical single-needle 'speaking' telegraph instrument as illustrated in ?yer & Co's 1874 booklet.
?uthor's collection

?bove (11):
?wo Saxby signalboxes of the mid-?860s straddling the South Eastern ?ailway's lines into London Bridge ?tation.
?llustrated London News, 8 September ?866, p 240

Stevens' 'Hook' lever frame of 1860 was manufactured until about 1870, and during that time it was installed by the Caledonian, Glasgow & South Western, Great Northern, Lancashire & Yorkshire, London, Chatham & Dover, London & South Western, North British, North Eastern and South Eastern Railways. To replace it Stevens patented in 1870 a lever frame with 'tappet' locking, (see Chapter 5, Part 2), a design which was destined to be manufactured in large quantities by all signalling contractors and railway company signalling departments, used by almost all the country's major railway companies, and which proved to be the most versatile type of mechanical locking ever invented. Tappet locking was often substituted for earlier forms when frames had to be re-locked as layouts changed.

The other major manufacturer to emerge in the 1860s was McKenzie, Clunes & Holland, established in Worcester in 1861. This firm (better known as just McKenzie & Holland after 1873), patented its first interlocking lever frame in 1866 (Patent No 1963), and after successfully defending a protracted court case (1869–1874) brought by Saxby & Farmer, emerged as one of that firm's major rivals in the 1870s.

8. Signalboxes or signal cabins — glazed structures developed by John Saxby, large enough to contain both interlocked lever frame and electrical equipment over which a signalman (or signalmen) had overall control. *(See photo 11)*

The way ahead, then, was persuading railway companies to combine all these elements to achieve safer operating practices.

INCENTIVES FOR CHANGE:
I) LEGISLATION

A significant incentive was the threat of legislation to force companies to conform to Board of Trade recommendations. When at the beginning of the 1870s this seemed a distinct possibility, the majority of the country's railways began to introduce the Block System, and with it a programme of interlocking. In 1871 the Regulation of Railways Act extended the Board of Trade's existing powers, ie the inspection of new lines before they opened to the public, to the inspection of alterations undertaken on existing lines. Given the Board's insistence on interlocking, and the inevitable expansion of track layouts because of growing traffic demands, this very effectively forced the pace of change. The Act also granted powers to the Board of Trade to investigate all railway accidents, publish reports of the findings and make recommendations for change, a practice which up until then had been by voluntary agreement. (It was the Royal Commission on Railway Accidents which organised the first trials to compare the performance of various braking systems on a stretch of the Midland Railway just south-west of Newark in 1875.)

Following the success of the 1871 legislation, the Board of Trade tried to introduce a bill compelling companies to fully interlock all their lines as well as adopt the Block System within five years. Although the capacity of contractors to manufacture and install new equipment was increasing at the time, it would have been impossible to meet this sudden demand, so in 1873 an Act was passed merely requiring every railway company to submit an annual return stating the progress made with interlocking and Block Signalling. The threat of further legislation if the returns did not show improvements was incentive enough for change. The same tactic was used to encourage railway companies to fit continuous automatic brakes to their engines and trains, when the Railway Returns (Continuous Brakes) Act was passed in 1878.

II) SIGNALLING CONTRACTORS (MECHANICAL)

At this crucial period when railway companies were demanding new mechanical devices and hundreds of wooden signal posts and arms, the necessary machine tools for cutting, planing, slotting, boring, and jointing both wood and metal to the necessary fine tolerances needed in interlocking frames and signals, were readily available. The art of blacksmithing was giving way to the art of machine tool operation at just the right time, as the 1870s also witnessed the addition of high quality steel to the list of useful materials.

All over the country new metal-working foundries sprang up to supply everything from cast iron manhole covers to agricultural machinery. Saxby & Farmer, Stevens & Son and McKenzie & Holland's virtual monopoly in the early 1870s of the supply and fixing of mechanical equipment (including signals and signalboxes), was challenged. Of the challengers only a few firms managed to establish a hold in this specialist market, the most successful being Easterbrook & Co, The Gloucester Wagon Co Ltd, I'Anson & Sons & Co, Ransomes & Rapier, J. Tweedy & Co and E S. Yardley & Co (later W. Smith) Nevertheless, competition drove prices down and consequently more railway companies were encouraged to upgrade their signalling.

Competition also encouraged the established contractors to improve their products, and during the same period, both Saxby & Farmer and McKenzie & Holland consolidated their reputations and their firms' strong financial positions with a number of new interlocking lever frames. Saxby & Farmer added two new designs to its range the 'Rocker' of 1871 (Patent No 1601) and more successful and widely used, the 'Rocker & Gridiron' of 1874 (Patent No 294). *(See photos 12 & 13)* Both frames acquired their names from the prominent curved plates in front of the levers which 'rocked' when the lever catch-handle was grasped. The 'rockers' were connected to the locking behind the levers. The first grasp of the catch-handle moved the appropriate locks to their first position, the 'rocker' then remaining in the same position whilst the lever was reversed preventing other levers from being moved. At the end of the lever's stroke when the catch handle was released, the 'rocker' was forced down, moving the locks to their second position thus locking or unlocking other levers This was really the first frame to successfully use the levers' catch-handles to operate the interlocking, in contrast to other designs in which the actual movement of the whole lever whilst in motion activated the locks. The advantage of 'catch-handle' locking over 'lever locking' was that in the latter, the force of a signalman pulling at a locked lever might distort or even override the locking if it was in direct contact with the lever, and certainly the locks tended to wear quickly. With 'catch handle locking', the only force exerted on the

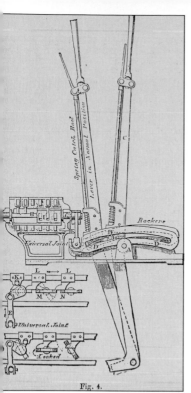

Fig. 4.

locks was the grasp of the signalman's hand.

In 1873 McKenzie & Holland introduced a new frame (Patent No 2034) with lever activated locking. The frame sold in large numbers and undoubtedly secured the firm's trading position until the turn of the century. During the period of the frame's manufacture up to the end of the 1880s, it went through a number of technical changes, but all subsequent designs inherited the 1873 frame's overall appearance. The most noticeable feature was that in their normal position the levers were vertical, but when reversed they were inclined forward quite dramatically compared with other types of frames.

Left (12):
Side elevation of Saxby & Farmer's 'Rocker & Gridiron' lever frame of 1874. *From, Safe Railway Working, Clement E. Stretton, 1887*

Below (13):
Detail showing how the 'rockers' of Saxby's 1874 frame were connected to the locking.
National Railway Museum collection

III) SIGNALLING CONTRACTORS (ELECTRICAL)

During the 1870s, the number of firms producing electrical equipment also blossomed to meet the demand for block instruments. The most common form were undoubtedly those derived from telegraph instruments, with single needles activated by continuous current, the standard needle movement in most being made to Spagnoletti's patent. The 'speaking' telegraph form of the instrument was used extensively by most railway companies, and the block instrument derivative by, amongst others, the GNR, LNWR, MS&LR, MR, North British and North Eastern Railways. Apart from the fact that the handle of the block instruments could be held over either to the right or left, and that 'line clear', 'line blocked' and 'train on line' were painted on the instrument dials, both block and telegraph instruments were identical in construction and electrical circuitry. In fact an unfortunate legacy of the single-needle block instrument's telegraph origins which was perpetuated in many of them, was the painting green of the

Below (14):
A Tyer's one-wire, two-position semaphore block instrument removed from the ex-London, Brighton & South Coast Railway signalbox at Crowborough in 1989.
Author's collection

backgrounds to the needle units. A black needle against a green background in a dimly lit signalbox must have been very difficult to see, yet companies like the MR and the NBR continued to use this colour scheme up to the end of their independent existence in 1923. A number of instruments lasted in their original state until the 1970s.

The firms which made these instruments are less appreciated than Tyers or Sykes (see below), and largely anonymous, although some of the surviving instruments are marked with their makers stamps:

Great Northern Railway:
>Harborow & Co, Circus Street, London
>Helsby Telegraph Works, Nr Warrington
>Reid Brothers, 12 Wharf Road, London

Manchester, Sheffield & Lincolnshire Railway, and Midland Railway:
>E.G. Bartholomew
>Blakey, Emmott & Co, Halifax

North British Railway, and North Eastern Railway:
>Brittan, London
>H. White & Co, London

The firm of Tyer & Co also marketed a single-needle telegraph instrument and eventually manufactured continuous current single-needle block instruments. But its reputation was founded on its one-wire instruments as described in Chapter 3, and in the fifth edition of its publicity booklet dated March 1874, it was able to boast that all the following railway companies had purchased and were using its equipment:

Bristol & Exeter (N)
Bristol & Portishead Pier
Caledonian (S)
Cambrian
Deeside
East London
Furness
Glasgow & South Western (S)
Great Eastern (N)
Great North of Scotland
Great Western   — West Midland
                    — Pontypool Road & Hereford
                    — Hirwain Summit & Glynn Neath Incline
                    — Neath Junction
                    — Tidal Bridges, Swansea
London & North Western (N)
London & South Western   —

Cosham & Portsmouth
London, Brighton & South Coast (S)
Monmouthshire
North British
North London
North Staffordshire
Taff Vale   — Yniscoi &
                                         Rhymney Junction
Whitehaven, Cleator & Egremont

Some of these companies favoured Tyer's instruments with needle indications, whilst others preferred 'line clear' and 'train on line' to be given by miniature semaphore arms instead. Where the companies' original preferences are known, 'S' indicates semaphore, and 'N' needle.

Such was the reliability of Tyer's instruments, and the loyalty of many of these companies to the firm's products, that many of their routes continued to be controlled by Tyer's block instruments until the 1980s. *(See photo 14)*

Of the other block instruments described in Chapter 3, the following were the companies using them, based on a list in W. E. Langdon's The Application of Electricity to Railway Working, published in 1897.

Preece	(one-wire & three-wire semaphore):
	Great Northern of Ireland
	Great Western
	Lancashire & Yorkshire
	London & South Western
	Midland & Great Western of Ireland
Spagnoletti	(three wire 'disc')
	Great Western
	Metropolitan
Walker	(one-wire semaphore)
	South Eastern
	London, Chatham & Dover
	North Eastern (Stockton & Darlington line)

V) IN-HOUSE MANUFACTURING

Although much new signalling work in the early years of the 1870s was undertaken by contractors, as the decade progressed a number of the larger railway companies already producing or just beginning to manufacture their own steam locomotives and rolling stock, decided to expand their new foundry, machine shop and woodworking facilities for the production of signalboxes and mechanical signalling equipment.

Just predating this trend, the SER was once again in the forefront of signalling

development when in 1867 its Engineer, Francis Brady, was granted a patent (No 1959) for a very neat and compact interlocking lever frame which continued to be manufactured until the late 1880s. The 'travel' or stroke of the levers was the shortest of any frame ever made, and the interlocking was also confined to an unusually small space just beneath the operating floor in front of the levers.

The GWR had manufactured some of its own signalling equipment at Reading from 1859, and the patent for a frame to the designs of the company's Engineer, M. Lane, was granted in 1865 (No 432). But it was not as successful as Brady's design and it was only in the 1870s that locking frames and signalboxes of purely Company designs were made in any quantity. The first successful frame was the 'Single Twist', so-called because the bars connected to the levers which drove the locking twisted during the lever stroke.

The GWR still had to employ contractors to fulfil all its signalling requirements in the 1870s, however, and so technically the first company to begin manufacturing in earnest, and to become totally self-sufficient, was the MR. Its activity coincided with the implementation of the decision to introduce the block system along its main lines. Right at the end of the 1860s the company designed and began to manufacture what were arguably the neatest interlocking lever frames of any contractor or other railway company.

All the cast and wrought-iron components could be easily handled and bolted together to create frames with any number of levers. Only the locking bars had to be tailor made for the layout the frame was to control. The locking was activated by the levers' catch-handles via cylindrical bars which, because they twisted when the catch-handles were operated, became known as 'tumblers'. The whole frame has thus acquired the name 'Midland Tumbler'. *(See photo 15)* When tappet locking was introduced into the frames from 1906 onwards, the external appearance changed very little, and the same overall appearance was carried over into British Railways days when in 1948 the last version of the design was adopted by the London Midland Region as its standard lever frame. All the locking was contained within the frame just behind the levers, which made it readily available for attention, and it also meant that signalbox interiors were not as draughty as those where the levers passed through the operating floor to the locking rooms beneath.

To house the new 'Tumbler' frames, the MR designed a number of standard prefabricated wooden sections that could be

made up into signalboxes of varying sizes and having once established the design, the style of MR signalboxes altered only subtly up to the Grouping of 1923.

The LNWR was the next company to begin to manufacture its own signalling equipment. The decision was taken in 1872, but it took some time before Saxby & Farmer ceased to have any involvement with the LNWR's signalling. Signalboxes designed at Crewe began to appear from 1874 onwards, and although the design evolved over the years, standard features such as windows with tall narrow panes gave the mainly brick-based structures a characteristically massive North Western appearance.

In February 1874 F. W. Webb of the LNWR was granted his first patent (No 442) for an interlocking lever frame, and as with the MR's equipment, it set the standard for all later company designs although details differed. As with the Midland frames, standard components meant frames of any number of levers could be assembled. But whereas MR frames were neat and elegant in all design details, from the catch-handles to the simple curved plates protecting the locking, Webb's equipment was in comparison both massive and yet brutally simple. The frames were probably more durable than most, but the gaps for the levers to penetrate into the locking room, for example, were larger than in any other frame, and consequently LNWR signalboxes could be draughty places. A further patent followed exactly a year later, (Patent No 462) and then in June 1876 a third was granted (Patent No 2352) which introduced a rocking plate into the frame to activate the locking similar in use to the 'rocker' in Saxby & Farmer's 1871 and 187? frames. To confuse matters this rocking plate was called a 'tumbler', though it bore no resemblance to the MR's mechanism of that name, and frames with this device have generally become known as 'Webb Tumbler' frames. They became the LNWR's standard frame and were manufactured in quantity until superseded by frames with tappet locking designed in 1903. *(See photos 16 & 17)* The LNWR also designed and manufactured its own block instruments and ancillary electrical equipment, but as these did not appear until the 1880s, they are examined in Chapter 5 Part 3.

Other companies never matched the output of mechanical signalling equipment or achieved the self-sufficiency of the MR and LNWR during the 1870s. The GNR, for example, made a few small frames in the first years of the decade but then used contractors exclusively until the 1880s. The MS&L designed its own lever frames which were made either by the company or by outside foundries in the early 1870s, but after 188? employed only contractors.

Above (15):
The 20-lever Midland Railway 'Tumbler' frame photographed in Edale signalbox in 1980. *Author*

Above opposite (16):
Part of the London & North Western Railway lever frame in Marsden Junction signalbox. Behind the levers is the 'pulling board' with various cast iron description plates. On the block shelf are four of the final form of Fletcher's standard double line block instruments with track circuit repeaters attached to the sides. To their left is a route indicator adapted from a single-needle pegging instrument. *BR*

Below opposite (17):
A gantry of London & North Western Railway lower quadrant signals at Kensington Addison Road just before World War 2. *C. R. L. Coles*

THE 1870S LEGACY

The legacy of the 1870s signalling 'revolution' was considerable. Because we are so used to seeing photographs of Britain's railways taken after World War 1, it must not be assumed that the signalling of the 1870s was as uniform and comprehensive as it was later, but although interlocking and the block system had not been universally adopted by the end of the decade, the change in operating attitudes all over the country was very noticeable. In 1875 63% of connections on passenger lines in England and Wales were interlocked with just 35% in Scotland; by 1880 those figures had risen to 82% and 64% respectively, with companies like the London, Brighton & South Coast and North Staffordshire Railways having a 100% record. In 1874 63% of double lines in England and Wales were controlled by the 'Absolute Block' system, (see Chapter 5) with 33% recorded for Scotland; by 1880 the returns were 89% and 71% respectively.

During the 1870s and 1880s, all the major railway companies developed their own distinctive style of signalbox and semaphores, which altered very little before the Grouping of 1923. Along with the locomotives and rolling stock, they stamped an unmistakable individual identity on each company, distinguishing the MR from the GNR in Lincoln, for example, or the GWR from the LSWR in Exeter. *(See photo 18)*

But the legacy of the 1870s also had two very significant negative effects, which were only really felt many years later. The first was that because so much faith was placed in the principles of mechanical interlocking and the block system, and because the fight had been so hard won by the Board of Trade, signalling philosophy did not progress *fundamentally* after the 1870s. The following decades witnessed considerable refinements to equipment and Rules & Regulations, but there were few innovations. For example, although all railway companies since the mid-1860s had agreed that distant signals performed a 'cautionary' role, it was not until 1925 that it was agreed to distinguish distant signals from 'stop' signals by painting the arms yellow and more importantly changing the 'caution' aspect from a red to a yellow light. And yet at exactly the same time as this 'third' aspect had been agreed, the Institution of Railway Signal Engineers, was formulating a completely new signalling philosophy around three- and four-aspect colour light signals (the basis of modern signalling) which would have been impossible without the yellow, third, aspect.

The second negative consequence of the 1870s signalling 'revolution' was arguably more destructive. Much of the equipment installed by railway companies between the 1870s and the turn of the century was never replaced. In 1962 when 'Deltic' diesel locomotives with a capacity for sustained 100mph sprinting took over all the expresses on the East Coast main line, there were still more than 100 manual signalboxes between King's Cross and Doncaster, many dating back to the 1870s. Most operated the block system with single-needle instruments of GNR origin and controlled their block sections with semaphore signals. The equipment had certainly stood the test of time, but by the 1960s the manning of thousands of signalboxes up and down the country, and the maintenance of thousands of ageing mechanical lever frames and thousands of block instruments, with all the staff implications, only helped make many branch lines and secondary main lines in particular appear very uneconomical to a Ministry of Transport run by Ernest Marples and fed statistics by Dr Beeching. Perhaps if modernisation had been implemented earlier, and signalling costs had been reduced, some of those lines might have been reprieved.

Above (18):
'B1' No 61188 passes the typical Great Northern Railway signalbox at Bottesford between Grantham and Nottingham in the 1950s.
T. G. Hepburn; Rail Archive Stephenson

PART 1: RULES AND REGULATIONS

Although the basic principles of the block system and interlocking were adopted generally, the immediate legacy of the 1870s signalling revolution was a wide diversity of operating practices between railway companies. As the 1880s progressed, a general consensus was reached partly by agreement, and partly as a result of Board of Trade intervention. But complete standardisation of Rules & Regulations, including terminology and bell codes, did not occur until almost the turn of the century.

THE BASICS

By the 1880s, the following principles were common to all railway companies:

1. Signalmen always controlled the block sections in rear of them. Any train approaching a signalbox on the correct line was approaching from the *rear*, and conversely any train going away from a signalbox on its correct line was in *advance* of that signalbox. A signalman always had to gain the permission of his colleague in advance before sending trains forward. A train was 'offered' forward, and either 'accepted' or 'refused'. Every signalbox was issued with its own clock, usually with a good quality chain fusee movement, and the types of message exchanged between signalmen on their block instruments and bells, and the time they were transmitted and received were recorded in a bound book — the 'train register' — up and down trains on separate pages. 'Train registers' had been used by the Great Northern and South Eastern Railways in the 1850s and were subsequently adopted by all

companies. In large and/or busy signalboxes one or more 'booking lads' were often employed just to keep the register up to date.

2. Each through line at every signalbox was protected by at least two semaphore signals — the 'home', a red stop signal, and — the 'distant', a red caution signal with a 'V' shaped notch cut out of the end. Every signal where possible was placed on the left-hand side of the line in the direction of travel, and was capable of displaying two indications — 'danger' and 'all clear' in the case of the home signal, and 'caution' and 'all clear' in the case of the distant signal. When the semaphores were at danger or caution they were termed 'on', and when at all clear they were considered 'off'. In many places an additional stop signal was provided in advance of the home signal — the 'starter' or 'starting', also a red stop signal. If a home signal only was provided at a signalbox, then that controlled entry into the block section; if a starter was provided, then that became the 'section signal'. The distant signal only gave a clear indication if all stop signals showed clear. Drivers were not expected to stop at distant signals at caution, but as its indications anticipated those of the home and starter, it naturally became an important signal for all drivers.

3. The block section on most lines was considered as extending from the outermost stop signal, either the 'home' or 'starter', of one signalbox, to the first stop signal of the next signalbox in advance. If a 'home' and 'starter' were provided, then the stretch of line between them was called by a number of companies the 'station limits.' *(See Fig 1)*

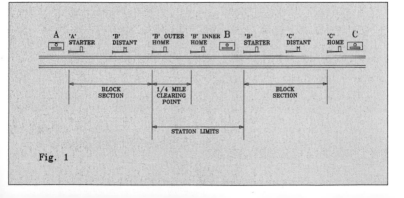

Fig. 1

'CLOSED' BLOCK WORKING

In the early 1870s the normal position of the semaphores and the block instruments controlling a block section was 'clear'. Only when a train passed through the section were the fixed signals returned to 'danger' and the block instrument indications altered to 'train on line.' Following an accident at Abbots Ripton on the GNR main line in 1876, when the semaphores had become frozen in the 'clear' position and could not be returned to danger, the Board of Trade recommended that semaphore signals should be maintained at 'danger' until permission had been obtained to allow a train through the block section. This in effect meant the block section was normally 'closed'. By the 1880s all railway companies using block working were operating their semaphore signals according to the new standard, although the principle of the closed block was not adopted on every line and took longer to be accepted.

In the case of railway companies using three-wire equipment, changing to a closed block system was achieved by using in a positive way the third indication possible on their block instruments — 'line blocked' — with the needle in the vertical position between 'line clear' and 'train on line', (the LNWR actually used the word 'closed' rather than 'blocked' on its three-position instruments). An added bonus when using continuous current instruments in this way was the saving of battery power, as 'line blocked' was indicated when no current was flowing. Unfortunately, this change had significant implications for companies using one-wire instruments, like those manufactured by Tyer & Co, which were designed electrically to give only two indications — see Part 3 of this chapter.

It is relevant at this point to mention that the Southern Railway's later use of the terms 'open' and 'closed' in relation to block working, carried different meanings to those outlined here — see Chapter 6.

ABSOLUTE AND PERMISSIVE BLOCK WORKING

In 1889, following the disaster at Armagh on the 12 June that year, when an ordinary passenger train sent ahead using the 'time interval' system ran into the rear of a packed excursion train killing 78 and injuring about 250, the legislation threatened in 1872/3 to make the block system compulsory for working all passenger lines, was enacted. The Armagh disaster was made worse by the lack of an automatic brake on the excursion train, and so the 1889 Regulation of Railways Act also required railway companies to fit all their passenger trains with continuous brakes that

would operate automatically if a train became divided. So great was the public outcry that the Act even managed to require all railway companies to fully interlock all their lines. In reality the Act merely hastened the inevitable. By the end of the 1880s, most companies had almost achieved what the legislation demanded, although there were interesting exceptions. For example, on the MS&LR's double-track line from Lincoln to Wrawby Junction (Barnetby), 'time interval' working was still in operation for 26 miles between Claytons Siding signalbox at Lincoln, and Howsham just south of Wrawby Junction. Nevertheless, full interlocking and block working with only minor omissions had been achieved throughout the country by 1895.

The 1889 Act actually stipulated the use of 'Absolute Block Working' on all lines carrying passenger traffic. This meant strictly enforcing the principle of allowing only one train at a time travelling in the same direction through a 'block section'. No train could follow another until the signalman at the place where the train exited from the section had communicated by block instrument that the line was clear for a following train.

The less restrictive form of block working whereby more than one train at a time travelling in the same direction could occupy a block section, favoured by companies like the LNWR and GNR before 1870, had developed by the 1880s into 'Permissive Block Working' and was mainly used on goods and slow lines — see Part 3 of this chapter.

TOWARDS STANDARDISATION

When it came to the Rules & Regulations, and the terminology used to implement block working, there were still significant differences between companies in the 1870s. At the end of 1874 a committee had been set up to try and improve a set of standard Rules & Regulations agreed by the General Managers' Conference of 1867, and the changes were approved in 1876. Still more needed to be achieved, however, as was tragically demonstrated when in December 1881 a series of accidents in Canonbury Tunnel within the space of an hour were caused because the seven-stroke bell code tapped out by the North London Railway signalman to signify 'line temporarily blocked' according to his Company's Regulations, was interpreted by the GNR signalman receiving them according to his Company's Regulations as permissive working. As a direct result of this misunderstanding, 17 basic bell codes, including, most importantly, emergency ones, were finally standardised and came into use between October and December 1884.

THE FIRST STANDARDS

For companies such as the GNR, NER, MS&LR and the MR, using three-wire systems with single-needle instruments and bells (including the GWR with its Spagnoletti 'disc' instruments), the following were the Railway Clearing House's 1884 bell codes and procedures. It is also interesting to note, that many single-line railways such as the Somerset & Dorset Joint Railway used the same codes and procedures.

BELL SIGNALS	
To Call Attention	1 beat
Train Entering Section or Train on Line	2 beats
Is Line Clear for Light Engine, Mineral or Goods Train (other than Express Goods), Ballast Train running short distance, Ballast Train requiring to stop in Section, or Platelayers' Lorry requiring to pass through Tunnel?	3 beats
Is Line Clear for Passenger, Break Down Van, Fish, Milk, or Empty Coaching Stock Train?	4 beats
Is Line Clear for Meat, Cattle, or Express Goods Train, or Ballast Train conveying workmen, or running long distance without stopping?	5 beats
Obstruction Danger Signal	6 beats
Stop & Examine Train	7 beats
Signal given in Error, Train last signalled not coming	8 beats
Train passed without Tail Lamp (to signalbox in advance)	9 beats
Train Divided	10 beats
Shunt Train for following Train to pass	11 beats
Train or Vehicles running away on wrong line	12 beats
Section Clear and Station or Junction Blocked	13 beats
Train or Vehicles running away on proper Line	14 beats
Opening of Signalbox	15 beats
Testing Bell Signal	16 beats
Closing of Signalbox	17 beats
Time Signal	18 beats

All the bell codes above, were transmitted one beat after another. Codes were not divided up into groups of beats with pauses in between. For example, if a signalman wanted to transmit 'Shunt train for following train to pass', then the eleven beats were tapped out consecutively

Photographs 19 a,b&c show block instruments of GNR origin. With minor differences, (the GNR used the terminology TRAIN ENTERED SECTION instead of TRAIN ON LINE), they were typical of three-wire three-position single-needle equipment used by other companies. The normal indication was with the needle vertical at LINE BLOCKED. LINE CLEAR was indicated when the top of the needle pointed to the right, and TRAIN ON LINE when the top of the needle pointed to the left. Assuming the instruments are in signalbox 'B' and signalbox 'A' is to the left:

When the signalman at 'A' wanted to send a train forward to 'B', he called the attention of the signalman at 'B' with one beat on the bell and after 'B' replied with one beat, 'A' offered him the train by tapping out the appropriate bell code.

a) If the signalman at 'B' was able to accept the train, he repeated the code and pegged his instrument to 'line clear'. This indication was repeated in signalbox 'A'. If 'B' was unable to accept the train then he simply ignored the message, which his colleague would continue to send at short intervals. At certain locations, if he already had a train standing just beyond his home signal, ('inside' in railway terminology), or at a junction had already accepted another train, then he could reply with 13 beats on the bell, which warned the signalman at 'A' to caution the train on entering the section. (This became Regulation 5 — see page 98) Once a 'line clear' had been given, the signalman at 'B' could not alter points or shunt another train on the line on which the train had been accepted.

b) When the train left 'A' and entered the section, the signalman there called the attention of 'B' again, and on receipt of an answer gave two beats on the bell. The signalman at 'B' repeated the code and then unpegged his block instrument. The signalman at 'A' then used the handle on his non-pegging instrument to send a 'dial signal' which consisted of a number of beats of the

needle either to the right or left, to confirm the type of train entering the section. After the dial signals had been exchanged the signalman at 'B' pegged his block instrument to 'train on line'. The signalman at 'B' then called the attention of 'C', described the train, and 'C' pegged a 'line clear' which was repeated on 'B's' non-pegger. 'B' could then pull his signals 'off' for the train to proceed to 'C'.

c) When the train reached 'B', had passed his outermost home signal, and the train was entering the forward section, the signalman at 'B' sent two beats on the bell to 'C'. Dial signals would be exchanged and 'C' would

Above (19a, b & c):
A typical arrangement of block instruments and single-stroke bells in a signalbox controlling a double line. The three instruments on the left communicate with signalbox 'A'; the three on the right with signalbox 'C'.

peg 'train on line'. 'B' then gave 'out of section' to his colleague at 'A' and unpegged the handle on his instrument so that the needle dropped to 'line blocked'. Surprisingly in the RCH list there was no bell code for 'out of section', although both the GNR and MR used two beats of the needle to the right in the code of dial signals to indicate this.

Although the bell codes were standard, the dial signals were not, so for example, five deflections of the needle to the left meant 'Line clear for Express Goods, Fish or Cattle etc' to a MR signalman, but 'On line for Mineral or Ballast train stopping at chief stations only' to a GNR signalman.

THE RAILWAY CLEARING HOUSE 1895 STANDARDS
The above procedures not only varied slightly between companies using single-needle block instruments and bells, but were different if a line was equipped with one-wire instruments. Obviously it was not practical to transmit complicated dial signals on one-wire instruments, and consequently complete standardisation of all Rules, Regulations and the terminology used when operating the block system was still elusive. Clement E. Stretton, Vice President & Consulting Engineer to the Amalgamated Society of Railway Servants drew attention to this dangerous lack of standardisation in his book, Safe Railway Working published in 1887, and by the beginning of the 1890s, the Board of Trade was pressing hard to achieve uniformity. Finally in 1893 a survey of all railway companies' terminology and procedures was undertaken, and the results compared against a set of RCH standards.

The findings of the survey led the RCH to issue a comprehensive set of 30 standard block regulations and 33 bell codes which were finally brought into operation on 3 March 1895. There followed 281 standard rules in 1904, both Rules & Regulations only being added to, not modified, to suit individual companies needs. They remained the standard until the 1980s.

The complexity and subtlety of these new standard Rules & Regulations reflected not only the increased complexity of the railway network and its operation at the turn of the century, but also the increased ability of the railway workforce to put them into practice. By this time the majority of railway employees were literate, articulate and capable of reasoned decision making under considerable pressure, a generation removed from the times when educated men like William Preece felt signalling devices and procedures needed to be as simple as possible to operate for staff with little or no formal education.

Complexity, nevertheless, needed explanation, and by the Grouping a number of companies had established signalling schools where trainee signalmen could learn the necessary skills with the aid of model railways, miniature lever frames and full size block instruments, bells, signal repeaters, etc. Eventually every signalman on Britain's railways passed through one of these schools.

BELL CODES
Of the many differing elements of block working that the 1893 survey revealed, and the changes that were made to the existing 1884 standard, the most significant are outlined here.

During the 1880s, a number of railway companies had begun to transmit their bell codes in groups of beats. The 1884 RCH standard codes could be similarly divided, and Stretton records in his 1887 book that the GWR used the following three beat codes:

a) three beats transmitted consecutively meant 'Ordinary goods, mineral, ballast train, or engine and brake.'
b) three beats transmitted as '1 pause 2' meant 'Branch goods train.'
c) three beats transmitted as '2 pause 1' meant 'Train arrived or obstruction removed', in other words 'Out of section.'

Most of the RCH 1895 standard codes were divided into groups of beats, although they were still referred to by the total number of beats. For example, the code for opening a signalbox was described as 15 beats on the bell, but was transmitted as '5 pause 5 pause 5.' In the new standard, an ordinary passenger train became '3 pause 1', whilst the code for a light engine became '2 pause 3' replacing the old RCH standard of just three beats, enabling three beats to be used exclusively for giving 'out of section' — '2 pause 1.'

On its Spagnoletti instruments, the GWR never used dial signals, and as they could not be transmitted easily on one-wire instruments, dial signals for the description of trains were abandoned after the 1895 standards had come into force. This led companies like the MR, for example, to resurrect the procedure for the exchanging of routeing information — see Part 3 of this chapter.

'LINE CLEAR' AND THE 'CLEARING POINT'
The 1893 survey had also noted the lack of agreement between companies as to when 'line clear' could be given. Where signalboxes were at least two miles apart, the normal procedure was to ask for a 'line clear' from the signalbox in advance when 'train on line' had been received from the signalbox in rear — as

described above. Where signalboxes were closer together, this procedure was not appropriate, and on some lines 'line clear' was sought from the signalbox in advance as soon as it had been given in rear. On other lines where signalboxes were less than a quarter of a mile apart, 'train out of section' had to be received from the signalman in advance before 'line clear' could be given in rear. In other situations, the signalbox in rear might be authorised to send the 'train approaching' bell code of '1 pause 2 pause 1' a few minutes before the train passed by, the signalman receiving this code then seeking a 'line clear' from the signalbox in advance.

The actual definition as to what constituted a line that was clear so that 'line clear' could be given, also varied between companies. On some lines the last train had to have passed the section signal and be 'on its way' before another could be accepted. GNR signalmen were instructed to send 'out of section' as soon as the last vehicle had passed the signalbox, but then along with LNWR, MS&LR, and MR signalmen they could not accept a following train and peg 'line clear' until the line was unobstructed for at least a quarter of a mile in advance of the outermost home signal, ie the first stop signal a driver approaching from the rear would encounter. The new RCH standard adopted this quarter of a mile 'clearance' which was incorporated into Regulation 4.

As with all Rules & Regulations there were qualifications and exceptions. In the case of Regulation 4, level-crossing gates within the 'clearing point' did not constitute an obstruction, and 'line clear' could be given when they were across the line - Regulation 28. Obviously the interlocking prevented the signals from being pulled 'off' until the gates had been closed across the road.

In other circumstances where the 'clearing point' was not available, a signalman might if authorised, accept a train under the 'Warning Arrangement', (Regulation 5). In this case the signalman in rear would keep his signals at danger until the train was at a stand at the home signal. He would then 'caution' the driver verbally, telling him that the line was only clear as far as the home signal in advance, then lower his signal and display a green handsignal.

To counteract the delays that might arise from this procedure, the practice grew up in a few places of providing an extra stop signal at least a quarter of a mile in rear of the home signal. The extra signal became the 'outer home', and as long as the line was clear between it and the home signal, the signalman there could accept a train with no restrictions.

SHUNTING WITHIN THE CLEARING POINT — BLOCKING BACK

If a train had to be shunted within the clearing point, then the signalman in rear would be asked to 'block back'. This was done by placing his block instrument to 'train on line' and exchanging the bell code '2 pause 4'. When the manoeuvre was completed '2 pause 1' would be exchanged and the 'train on line' indication unpegged. If a train had to be shunted outside the home signal, the same procedure was carried out but with the exchange of the bell code '3 pause 3'.

In certain locations permission was given to shunt beyond the section signal into the forward section, the signalman in advance pegging his block instrument to 'train on line' after the exchange of the 3 pause 3 pause 2 bell code. The problem with this form of shunting was that the train was beyond the control of a stop signal, and a lapse on the part of the driver, might lead him to take the train completely through the section. To prevent this many railway companies adopted special shunting signals under the main stop signal, (see Part 2 of this chapter), or erected 'advanced starter' signals to extend the 'station limits', obviating the need to involve the signalman in advance.

PART 2: MECHANICAL DEVELOPMENTS

THE STOP SIGNAL

During the 1870s, double-arm semaphore signals at stations were the rule, and even into the 1880s they could still be found controlling block sections. However, as the block system became ever more sophisticated, their limitations became difficult to tolerate. When one of the semaphores was at 'danger', an engine driver had to know exactly where to stop his train without obstructing points and/or fouling other train movements. This was particularly dangerous at junctions. It was obviously far safer to provide separate signals so that drivers knew they had to stop just in front of — 'outside' in railway terminology — the relevant signal. It must have been particularly difficult for drivers approaching some of London's major termini protected by Saxby's elevated signalboxes with numerous double semaphores sprouting through their roofs. In areas where traffic was heavy, it was operationally better to have a number of closely spaced 'stop' signals to keep the trains moving, signal to signal. Gradually through the 1880s the single home signal was joined by other stop signals, known by different names on different lines but commonly referred to as, the 'inner home', 'outer home', 'starter', and 'advanced starter.'

SLOTTING

Where signalboxes were close together, two complications arose from the increasing number of stop signals. Firstly, the home signal of one signalbox might be in the place where the other signalbox's starter ought to be, and secondly the distant signal of one signalbox might coincide with the position of another signalbox's home or starter.

In the first case, one semaphore arm could act as both the home signal of one signalbox and the starter of the signalbox in rear. However, it was crucial that both signalmen should have to reverse the levers controlling the relevant semaphore before it would show a 'clear' indication and that if either signalman put his lever back to 'normal' in the frame, the semaphore would return to 'danger'. To achieve this, slots were formed at the bottom of the rod which ran up the side of the signal post from the balance weight to the arm. Three balance weights were required. One was attached to the main rod, whilst the others were each controlled by the two signalmen. The latter balance weights were attached to bars which passed through the slots. When both signalmen had reversed their levers, thereby pulling the bars of the balance weights down in the slots, the weight on the main rod pushed the semaphore arm into the 'clear' position. When either of the signalmen pushed their lever back into the frame, the balance weight bar dropped, pulling the main rod down, and thereby pulling the semaphore arm to 'danger'. Over the

years, other arrangements were devised to achieve the same result, but the terminology 'slotting' persisted as a description of all the various mechanisms.

Where the distant signal of one signalbox coincided with the position of another signalbox's home or starter, the distant signal of the signalbox in advance was usually positioned under the home signal of the signalbox in rear, and in certain circumstances if the latter signalbox also controlled a starter, an additional distant signal controlled by the signalbox in advance might be positioned under that as well. The 'slotting' arrangement was slightly different to that just described. The signalman in advance might pull his distant signal 'off', but if the home or starting signal above it on the post was still 'on', then the distant would also remain 'on'. Only when the home or starter had been pulled 'off' would the distant signal also clear. The distant signal could be returned to 'danger' whilst the home or starter remained 'off', but if the home or starter were returned to danger with the distant signal still 'off', then the slotting arrangement would cause both arms to be returned to danger. *(See fig 2)*

In both these examples, the 'slotting' mechanisms were in addition to the locking in the signalboxes' frames. Where signalboxes were closely spaced, many running line semaphores might be slotted, especially if distant signals under stop arms did not provide safe braking distances.*(See fig 3)* If

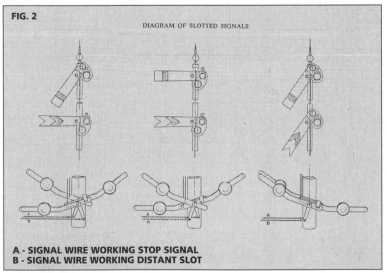

FIG. 2

DIAGRAM OF SLOTTED SIGNALS

A - SIGNAL WIRE WORKING STOP SIGNAL
B - SIGNAL WIRE WORKING DISTANT SLOT

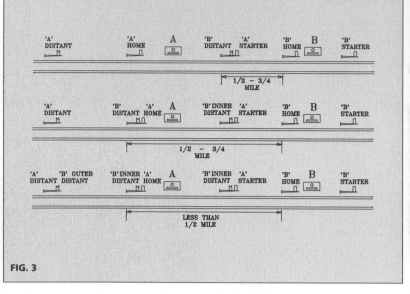

FIG. 3

the arrangement was complicated or signalmen could not see the arms responding to the lever, mechanical and electrical repeaters would be provided to indicate the state of the 'slots'. Some companies avoided complex slotting mechanisms by using such indicators. For example, a signalman might be instructed not to pull a certain signal 'off' until the indicator showed that the adjacent signalman had correctly cleared his signals. On the GWR if the line was clear to the clearing point but the signalman was not in a position to lower his signals, the bell code 2 pause 2 pause 2 would be sent in reply to a request for 'line clear'. After repetition, the signalman in rear would not pull his stop signals 'off' until the train had passed his distant in the 'on' position. In this way, the speed of the train could be effectively checked.

JUNCTION SIGNALS

Once the practice of mounting signals on top of the roofs of signalboxes had been abandoned, it became the accepted convention at junctions for the home signals controlling the diverging routes to be placed next to each other on separate posts mounted on top of a single post — in railway terminology a 'bracket'. The branch line home signal would invariably be on the shorter of the two posts, in other words the most important route, the main route, was protected

by the highest signal. If the diverging routes were considered of equal importance, both signals would be the same height. There were, of course, exceptions to these two conventions. Junction signals might consist of two separate posts side by side, one usually slightly shorter than the other.

Where the necessary number of posts and arms could not be accommodated on to one bracket, gantries were erected which often straddled a number of lines. The relative height of the posts once again signified relative importance, and if there were a number of routes involved, the semaphores reading from left to right controlled the routes geographically from left to right. Gantries very often carried signals for both 'up' and 'down' lines as well as signals applying to more than one line going in one direction, eg 'up' main line with 'up' goods and 'up' slow adjacent. *(See photo 20)* In the latter example, it was the driver's local knowledge that prevented him responding to the wrong signal.

The practice of mounting semaphore arms above each other at junctions on main lines where the highest arm controlled the most important route, was abandoned in the 1870s, (although there were exceptions, notably on the GNR), but the stacking of arms continued to be used in sidings, where the semaphores from top to bottom controlled sidings from left to right. *(See photo 21)*

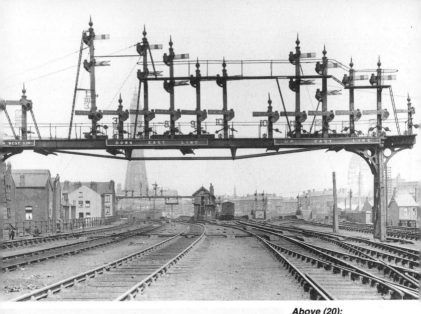

Above (20):
A gantry of Lancashire & Yorkshire Railway signals controlled from Blackpool Central signalbox, 1921.
National Railway Museum; HORF3188

Left (21):
Five Lancashire & Yorkshire Railway subsidiary signals controlled from Blackpool Central signalbox.
National Railway Museum; HORF3190

SPLITTING DISTANTS

To give drivers advanced warning of which route at a junction was set for them, and whether the controlling home signal was 'on' or 'off', most companies provided 'splitting distants'. For each diverging through route, there was a distant signal. *(See Fig 4)* These could be mounted on brackets or gantries exactly like their home equivalents, with the height of the post and the position from left to right carrying the same meanings as with the home signals. *(See photo 22)* Distant signals were not normally provided for controlling entry into sidings.

'Splitting distants' were not meant to be interpreted as speed signals. If a driver saw the distant 'off' for the secondary route at a junction, this was not an indication that the junction could be taken any faster than normal. Any speed restriction through that junction still had to be observed. Nevertheless, there were incidents arising from drivers taking junctions too quickly, and as a result in certain locations splitting distants were fixed at 'caution'. 'Fixed distants' were also used under stop signals to warn drivers that the next stop signal would invariably be in the 'on' position. By the turn of the century some companies were actively removing existing splitting distants, and by nationalisation it was no longer standard practice to provide them.

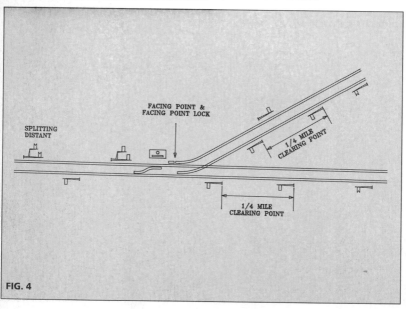

SPLITTING DISTANT

FACING POINT &
FACING POINT LOCK

1/4 MILE
CLEARING POINT

1/4 MILE
CLEARING POINT

FIG. 4

LAMPS, SPECTACLES AND SEMAPHORE ARMS

The lamps of early semaphore signals were usually fixed lower down the post than the semaphore arm itself. When the rod pushed the arm to one of its three positions, connecting rods would either rotate the whole lamp or just the coloured glasses within the case to alter the aspect. An alternative to this arrangement which eventually superseded it, was to place in front of the lamp a cast iron frame in which there was a red and blue coloured glass — in railway terminology a 'spectacle'. The spectacle was pivoted at right angles to the post and connected to the rod operating the semaphore arm. When the signal was at 'danger', the red glass was in front of the lamp; when at 'caution' the blue glass was in front of the lamp which, burning with a yellowish flame, projected a green light; and when the arm was in the post (all clear), the spectacle and its glasses were pushed away from the lamp so that the lamp's natural (technically white) light would be displayed. When two-position semaphores became the norm following the introduction of the block system, most semaphores continued to use revolving lamps or pivoted spectacles some with only a red glass in them.

Another legacy of the three-position semaphore was the pivoting of the semaphore arm in a slot in the post. Then in 1876, as every book on railway accidents and railway signalling relates, at Abbots Ripton on the GNR, snow packed into the slots of the signals showing clear and led directly to a series of fatal accidents. The result for the GNR was the gradual introduction of a

Above opposite (22):
Midland Railway lower quadrants (with corrugated steel arms) at Hendon. On the left, home signal with slotted distant signal beneath, and to the right a splitting distant.
Photomatic

Above and right (23a&b):
A Great Northern Railway somersault distant signal at Breadsall.
a) 'on'.
b)'off'. Above the cast iron bracket on which the arm is pivoted, is the rod connecting the arm to the spectacle. The other rods visible connected to the electrical contact box to the left of the spectacle, alter the indication of the signal repeater in Breadsall signalbox.
W. H. A. Thompson & D. J. Powell Collection

completely new design of signal in which the arm was pivoted centrally on a cast iron bracket about 3ft long protruding at right angles from the main post. To give a 'clear' indication the arm still assumed a vertical position, but in this new design it was parallel with, rather than inside, the post. As the arm remained visible in this position, it was the first semaphore to give a positive 'all clear' indication. Because of its acrobatic manoeuvre from 'danger' to 'clear', the new signal was christened a 'somersault', or to the ordinary signalman, a 'tumbler'. *(See photos 23a&b)* Following the GNR's lead, other companies began to abandon slotted post semaphores, whilst at the same time adopting a positive 'clear' indication with the arm lowered at 45°, the former 'caution' indication. Not all companies replaced their signals in such a fundamentally new way as did the GNR, however, favouring arms pivoted on, but not in, the post, instead. The main exception to this change was the North Eastern Railway, which continued doggedly right up to the end of its independent existence in 1922, to erect signals with arms in slotted posts both wooden and metal lattice.

The great advantage of mounting the semaphore arm outside the post, was that it was then possible to incorporate the spectacle into the end of the arm, and this change was implemented on most companies during the 1880s. This sensibly brought the daylight indication (the arm) physically in line with the night time indication (the lamp) which must have helped drivers when sighting signals. *(See photo 24)* More importantly, perhaps, making the spectacle part of the semaphore arm also improved its 'fail safe' qualities. In the event of the wire connecting the lever with the rod operating the semaphore arm breaking, it was important that the signal, no matter what aspect it was showing at the time, should 'fail' in the 'danger' position, in other words 'fail safe'. The weight of the rod connected to the arm and any counterbalance weights were sufficient to achieve this. But if the arm became detached from its rod, then it might easily fall into the 'clear' position. Adding the cast iron spectacle to the arm neatly solved this problem. On 'somersault' signals, of course, this was not possible, but as the

central pivot of the arm was offset vertically, the arm would balance in the horizontal plain if it became detached from the rod or weights at the bottom of the post. Nevertheless, the GNR continued until World War 1 to erect signals with the spectacle and lamps many feet lower down the posts than the semaphore arms, which complicated the rodding arrangement.

Most semaphore arms were wooden and varied in length from 6ft to 1ft long (the latter used in spaces with restricted clearance), but the normal length was about 5ft. The balance weights, spectacle and a physical stop kept the arm in the horizontal — 'danger' — position, but the 'clear' position could vary as wires contracted or expanded in different temperatures. Some early lever frames had ratchets along the stroke of the lever so that the length of stroke could be varied, according to the weather conditions, to maintain the semaphore arm's preferred angle and to make sure the glass in the spectacle lined up correctly with the lamp. More common were wire adjusters behind the levers, in a variety of styles, but all designed to adjust the tension on the wire connecting levers with the semaphores they controlled. Many companies quantified the margin of error in a certain number of degrees between an arm being considered 'on' or 'off'.

From the 1860s, the LNWR had attached rings to the semaphore arms of signals controlling goods or slow lines to distinguish them from main line signals, and many companies adopted this idea subsequently. Rings on subsidiary arms were still to be seen on former GWR lines into the 1980s. When the GNR adopted this approach after the Abbots Ripton disaster it also abandoned white light as a 'clear' indication in favour of green for main running lines, and introduced purple as the 'all clear' indication on goods and slow lines. This was in direct contrast to the LNWR, for example, which used purple in its shunting, ground, and bay starting signals to signify 'danger' or 'stop'. Gradually through the 1880s the LNWR also introduced the green aspect as the 'all clear' indication, and then in 1887 when the GNR decided to remove rings from its goods and slow line signals, it also abandoned the purple 'all clear' aspect.

As these changes were implemented, there was the real danger of misunderstandings, especially if drivers from one company had to run over the lines of another. For example, although green was gradually becoming the accepted 'all clear' signal for a number of companies, a white light still indicated 'all clear' on most lines, except on the GNR where drivers were specifically instructed to consider any display of a white light where a green or purple light ought to be displayed as a 'danger' signal.

These differences could not be tolerated as inter-company running and the speed and frequency of trains increased, and so at a Railway Clearing House meeting in July 1893, it was recommended that only two aspects should be adopted for all running line signals (both stop and distant signals) — red for 'danger', (or 'caution' on distant signals), and green for 'all clear'. Inevitably, it took some time before all companies implemented this recommendation but during this period of transition the vigilance and professionalism of footplate crews kept the trains running safely.

Unfortunately, the problems faced by crews trying to respond to faint paraffin lamps whilst travelling on rocking footplates with smoke periodically obscuring the view ahead, were not made any easier by the use of just two aspects for all signals. At night, stop signal indications were identical to distant signal ones, yet the meanings were obviously different. A driver needed to 'know the road' intimately so as not to confuse distant and stop signals. Yet despite this fundamental weakness which was potentially very dangerous, only three companies attempted to distinguish their distant and stop signals — the London, Brighton & South Coast, London

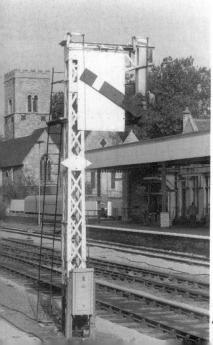

& South Western and the Furness Railways. The latter tried a flashing light on some of its distant signals, but the device used by the LB&SCR and the LSWR was known as the Coligny-Welch lamp. By means of an angled mirror inside the lamp case, an external screen, adjacent to the lens and just to the right of the spectacle frame, displayed a white chevron or arrow when the lamp was lit.

Another important comment in the 1893 RCH recommendations, was that at night when a semaphore was at 'danger', if it faced away from the signalman, it should display a small white light — in railway terminology a 'back light'. When the signal was pulled 'off', this light should be obscured to indicate that the arm had assumed the intended 'all clear' position. The 'back light' also had a very important 'fail safe' meaning, as well. If the signal lever was in the normal position, but the back light could not be seen, then either the signal lamp had become extinguished and needed attention, or the arm had fallen to the 'all clear' position and was giving a false indication.

SUBSIDIARY SIGNALS

Almost as soon as the semaphore had become the most common form of signal, engineers had attempted to give the arm a clear background so that its indication could not be misinterpreted and it could be seen from as great a distance as possible. This sometimes meant fitting a white board behind the arm, *(See photo 25)* or if the signal was next to a bridge, painting a white panel on the brickwork to highlight the arm. But the most common approach was to try to give the arm a clear background of sky, and this led to the erection of very tall posts on many lines. Such posts, at first wooden and then by the turn of the century more commonly metal lattice, appeared on almost every company at sometime, but perhaps the GNR is best remembered for having more than its fair share of extremely tall posts.

One of the problems with tall posts, however, arose when a driver had to stop just 'outside' them, and then might not be able to judge from his position immediately below whether the arm had come 'off' or not. The solution was to fix another arm at something like eye level, lower down the post, the two arms working together — 'co-acting'. Where 'co-acting' arms were fitted, sometimes only the lower arm had a spectacle attached. *(See photo 26)*

Occasionally, signals might be obscured by bridges, station buildings or be out of sight around a corner in a cutting. The latter problem was sometimes alleviated by placing the signal on the 'wrong' side of the line, but

by the turn of the century when electrical devices were becoming more acceptable, some companies used 'banner repeaters'. The most common of these were manufactured by W. R. Sykes and consisted of a centrally pivoted rectangular black board against a white background, behind glass in a circular cast iron case just over 2ft in diameter. The 'banner repeater' would be located some yards in rear of the signal to which it applied, and when that signal was 'on' the board was horizontal, and when 'off' the board was tipped down at 45°. At night the white background was illuminated. *(See photo 27)* If the repeater applied to a distant signal, then the left-hand end of the board was notched.

By the 1880s more use was being made of 'subsidiary' signals to control shunting movements. Like running signals they gave two indications, but their actual forms and the terminology used to describe them, differed according to the individual companies employing them. The nearest to a standard were the miniature semaphores, literally smaller versions of running signals, used in goods yards or beneath main stop signals to give 'calling-on', or 'shunt ahead' indications. When used as 'calling-on' signals, they indicated to a driver, according to local regulations, that the line was clear to a certain point and no further, or that although a platform was occupied by another train it could be entered with caution. 'Shunt ahead' signals tended to be placed under the signal controlling entry into a forward section, to indicate that the signal could be passed for shunting purposes only. Some companies actually attached a large letter 'S' to the arms to distinguish their use.

The greatest variety was evident in the case of 'ground' signals. As the name implies they were rarely more than a few feet above

Opposite (25):
An ex-Great Northern Railway lattice post bracket with sighting board photographed at Lincoln Central station in 1990. The post used to be in line with the station canopy and therefore the arm (originally a somersault) had to be cantilevered out in this way.
Author

Above right (26):
The co-acting down home signal of London, Brighton & South Coast Railway design at Faygate in 1959.
J. Scrace

Above left (27):
A Sykes 'banner repeater' on the Severn Valley Railway just outside Bewdley, 1994.
Author

the ground, and usually protected single points. They could take the form of either miniature arms but much smaller than those described above, or discs with or without an arm painted on them. The miniature arms performed exactly like their full-size equivalents, but the discs would operate in a number of different ways. They might rotate complete with their lamp to change indications; the lamp might remain static while the disc moved to position a different coloured glass in front of the lamp lens; or a flap might be pulled down in front of the lamp to display another aspect. On some lines ground signals were called 'dummies', and on others they were christened 'dollies', and as if reflecting this individuality in name, there was no real standard in design either until well into the 1930s.

ROUTE INDICATORS

By the turn of the century instead of using a plethora of arms on gantries to control diverging routes into sidings and platforms, a number of companies adopted 'route indicators' where trains approached at low speeds. Where there might have been half a dozen or more arms on a bracket or gantry, for example, just one home signal was erected with a large screen mounted beneath the arm capable of displaying numerals or letters corresponding to the appropriate siding or platform. When the signalman pulled any one of the home signal levers controlling entry into these sidings or platforms, the single semaphore arm would clear and in the screen one of the panels would appear displaying the appropriate letter or numeral. *(See photo 28)*

FOGMEN

Under normal circumstances, all railway signals were visual ones, whether flags, semaphore arms or lighted lamps shining through coloured glasses. What compromised visual signals was thick fog and falling snow. By the 1880s during this type of weather, signalmen on most railway companies had a fixed marker a set distance from their signalbox, which if it became obscured meant the services of at least two fogmen had to be called for. Each was then stationed at the distant signals to place detonators on the track when the signal was 'on', and remove them when the signal was pulled 'off'. In some locations 'fogging machines' of various types were used to place detonators on the line. Where it was difficult for the fogman to hear the signal being cleared, a 'dwarf signal' would be provided near to the foot of the post, often nothing more than a metal frame on which was pivoted a metal arm connected to the signal rodding. *(See photos 29 & 30)*

THE LEVER FRAME

Saxby's first lever frames separated the point levers from those which operated the signals, although all were arranged in a straight line with the connecting interlocking beneath the operating floor in the locking room or behind the levers. The 'travel' of the point and signal levers also differed, the 'travel' being the distance the lever had to be pulled from its 'normal' position, upright in the frame, to its 'reversed' position, angled towards the signalman. *(See photo 8)* By the 1870s the separation of levers by use was old-fashioned, but a number of frames, most notably those built by Stevens, still had different travels for levers operating points and signals.

By the 1880s it was usual for levers controlling 'up' line signals and points to be at one end of a frame, and those controlling 'down' line equipment to be at the opposite end. Distant signals tended to be the first and last levers in the frame, with the appropriate stop signals next to them. This general rule was modified slightly when there were levers controlling level crossing or wicket gates, which were normally next to the wheel operating them at one end of the frame. Some of McKenzie & Holland's later frames had the gate wheel actually built into one end. Another exception to the grouping of levers for 'up' and 'down' lines, was to be seen on the MR in the 1870s and 1880s. In the first 'tumbler' frames, levers were grouped geographically, with all the points and signals on one side of the signalbox being operated by the levers nearest that end regardless of whether they were for 'up' or 'down' lines, and vice versa. This sounds logical, until you realise that if a signalbox was equipped with starter, home and distant, the signalman was forever walking from one end of the frame to the other when he had to pull off for a through train.

Common to all frames was locking which prevented a signalman from pulling his distant signal until all the stop signals had been lowered, and forced him to place it back to the 'on' position before the stop signals could be returned to 'danger'. The order in which the

Opposite left (28):
Illuminated 'route indicator' at Southport station, Lancashire & Yorkshire Railway, 1919. *National Railway Museum; HORF2908*

Opposite right (29):
Midland Railway 'fogging machine' at Chinley in 1963. The detonators were either placed on, or removed from, the track by turning the wheel. Behind the wheel is the dwarf signal connected to, and repeating the indications of, the distant signal. *John Clarke*

Above (30):
A 'detonator placer'. In this particular example at Scout Green, Westmorland, it worked in conjunction with the home signal. When at 'danger' the detonators were positioned on the rail; when pulled 'off', the detonators were removed. *G. Clarke*

stop signals were pulled 'off' seems to have varied between companies. In British Railways days the accepted sequence was to clear the stop signals in the order in which an approaching train would encounter them — eg 'outer home', 'inner home', 'starter' and 'advanced starter'. This 'sequential locking' was usually part of the electrical interlocking connected with track circuiting — see Chapter 6.

As soon as Saxby and Stevens had begun to manufacture multi-lever frames, it was necessary to attach a number (either brass or cast iron) to each lever, linking its function to a diagram of the track layout hung above the lever frame. Sometimes the plate carrying the lever's number also listed one or more other numbers, to remind the signalman which levers had to be reversed beforehand. What the lever operated was then usually marked on a 'pulling board' which ran the full length of the frame behind the levers, at floor level, or sometimes immediately behind the catch-handles. These boards, mostly wooden, could be painted and hand lettered, or have individual engraved brass or cast iron plates attached. Some contractors and railway companies favoured a complete brass or cast iron plate. The more permanent the preferred option, the more inflexible it proved as layouts and lever functions changed.

On the MR's first frames engraved brass plates just over a foot long were attached to the right-hand side of each lever with a description of the signal or point it controlled.

(See photo 31) Later frames had this information displayed on square brass plates fixed immediately behind each lever.

The GNR was the first to use cast iron plates incorporating the lever's number, the piece of equipment it operated, and a list of the numbers of other levers in the locking sequence.*(See Fig 5)* This dispensed with the need for a pulling board. Some of the plates had numbers and words cast into them, but others had flat surfaces onto which the relevant information could be hand-lettered. *(See photo 32)* This form of lever plate became standard on the LNER, (eventually superseded by engraved plastic plates), and was also adopted by the Southern Railway which mounted the plates on the levers just above floor level.

All railway companies painted levers different colours to distinguish their use, but a complete standard was not agreed until the Grouping — see Chapter 6.

By the turn of the century, a number of companies had begun to fit new lever frames in signalboxes opposite the windows overlooking the running lines. This was supposed to give the signalmen a better view

Below (31):
Some of the brass description plates on the Midland Railway 'Tumbler' lever frame in Langham Junction signalbox.
W. H. A. Thompson & D. J. Powell Collection

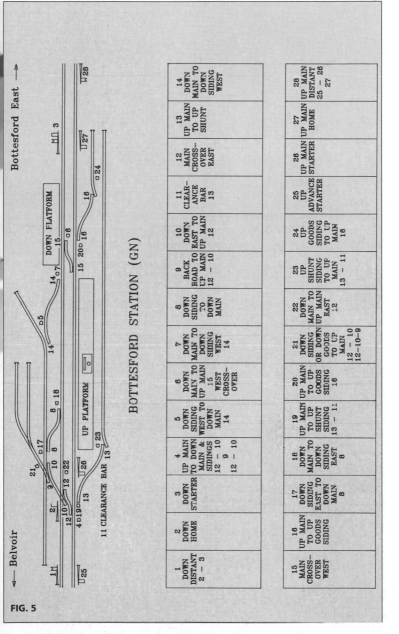

← Belvoir   Bottesford East →

BOTTESFORD STATION (GN)

FIG. 5

1 DOWN DISTANT 2 - 3	2 DOWN HOME	3 DOWN STARTER	4 UP MAIN TO DOWN MAIN & SIDINGS 12 - 9 - 10 12 - 10	5 DOWN SIDING WEST TO DOWN MAIN 14	6 DOWN MAIN TO UP MAIN 15 WEST CROSS- OVER	7 DOWN MAIN TO DOWN SIDING WEST 14	8 DOWN SIDING TO DOWN MAIN	9 BACK ROAD TO UP MAIN 12 - 10	10 DOWN MAIN EAST TO UP MAIN 12	11 CLEAR- ANCE BAR 13	12 MAIN CROSS- OVER EAST	13 UP MAIN TO UP SHUNT	14 DOWN MAIN TO DOWN SIDING WEST

15 MAIN CROSS- OVER WEST	16 UP MAIN TO UP GOODS SIDING	17 DOWN SIDING EAST TO DOWN MAIN 8	18 DOWN MAIN TO DOWN SIDING EAST 8	19 UP MAIN TO UP SHUNT SIDING 13 - 11	20 UP MAIN TO UP GOODS SIDING 16	21 DOWN SIDING OR DOWN MAIN UP MAIN GOODS TO UP MAIN 12 - 10 12-10-9	22 DOWN MAIN TO UP MAIN EAST 12	23 UP SHUNT SIDING TO UP MAIN 13 - 11	24 UP GOODS SIDING TO UP MAIN 16	25 UP ADVANCE STARTER	26 UP MAIN STARTER	27 UP MAIN HOME	28 UP MAIN DISTANT 25 - 26 27

of the lines under their control, but often the train register desk, noticeboard, the signalmens' wooden lockers, and a stove hindered the view as effectively as a row of levers and block instruments.

NEW FRAME DESIGNS
In the last two decades of the 19th century a number of new mechanical lever frames came onto the market produced by established and new independent signalling manufacturers. Those railway companies already manufacturing their own equipment brought out new designs, whilst others began to design and/or produce for the first time.

The new independent firms included — the Railway Signal Company (1881), Dutton & Co (1888) and Evans, O'Donnell (1894). Of these three, the Railway Signal Co gradually became a dominant force amongst established firms. It was formed by George Edwards who, after being promised all the Lancashire & Yorkshire Railway's signalling work, left the Gloucester Wagon Co to set up his own business. This monopoly provided the firm with a solid foundation, and the GNR, GER, and M&GNR railway companies, amongst others, all patronised the firm. At the end of the 1890s the company outbid the established firms to supply all the mechanical

equipment and signalboxes for the Manchester, Sheffield & Lincolnshire Railway's London Extension, and its success continued after World War 1, with the LNER as a major client.

The older firms replied with new frame designs of their own. During this period, the London, Brighton & South Coast, the South Eastern and the Great Central Railways had their own lever frame designs manufactured for them, whilst the Lancashire & Yorkshire, Cheshire Lines Committee and the North London Railways began to design and manufacture their own equipment. Between 1890 and 1908, the GWR added four new designs to its range, whilst the LNWR and MR simply modified their existing design to incorporate a different form of locking.

The form of locking that every company and signalling firm chose in the first decade of the 20th century was 'tappet' locking. In practical terms there was no choice, for two main reasons:

1. locking had become more sophisticated, and more use was being made of 'conditional' locking, ie one lever was not simply locked by another, but might be locked or free depending on the position of a set of levers.

2. the size of lever frames had increased so much that mechanical locking had reached the limits of its efficiency, and of all the types invented since the 1860s and 1870s, 'tappet' locking was the only design capable of coping with the complexity of mechanical frames both large and small. Once the limit of tappet locking had been reached in the first decade of the 20th century, the only way forward if more sophistication was demanded, was to use electrical locking.

TAPPET LOCKING

In its simplest form, tappet locking can be described as follows. A long flat bar (the tappet) approximately 1.5in or 2in wide was connected to each lever, usually below the operating floor. All the tappets were arranged parallel to each other, and passed through trays containing a number of smaller bars (locking bars) arranged at right angles to them. Depending on which lever had to lock or unlock another, the locking bars with shaped pieces of steel (the locks) at either end, were connected to each other. The shape, and position of the locks, coincided with similar shaped notches — 'ports' — cut into the tappet bars. As a lever was reversed, the lock was forced out of its port, moving the locking bar and thus pushing the lock at the opposite end of it into or out of a port on the tappet of another lever, depending on whether it had to be locked or unlocked by the first lever's movement. If the locking was between adjacent levers, no locking bar was necessary, the length of the steel lock being sufficient to make the connection. If a lever had to lock or unlock a number of other levers, then the tappet attached to it would have a number of ports cut into it, to displace a number of locking bars and locks. (See Fig 6) In large frames, each lever might have more than one tappet attached to it, and there might be two or more levels of locking trays.

POINTS

In most circumstances, each point was operated by its own lever, but in the case of 'crossover roads', ie trailing points connecting 'up' and 'down' lines on ordinary double lines, most companies used only one lever, except the LNWR which often used two.

As mentioned earlier, in the Glasgow & Edinburgh Rules & Regulations book of 1842, it was stated that all points along that company's main line had to be padlocked in the normal direction of travel. The fear of facing points altering their position whilst a train was crossing them persisted long after equipment had been developed which almost eliminated this risk and facing points were comparatively rare on running lines.

At junctions and large stations facing points could not be avoided and consequently, as interlocking lever frames developed in the 1860s and 1870s, so too did facing point locks (FPL). For every facing point lever, there was an adjacent facing point lock lever, which operated a bolt (sometimes called a 'plunger') locking the point blades in whichever position the signalman had set them, and preventing the point lever from

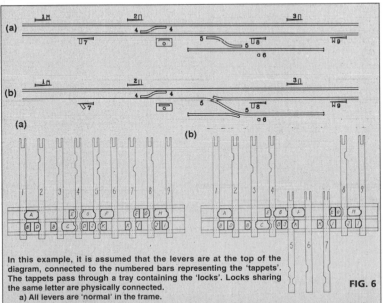

In this example, it is assumed that the levers are at the top of the diagram, connected to the numbered bars representing the 'tappets'. The tappets pass through a tray containing the 'locks'. Locks sharing the same letter are physically connected.

FIG. 6

a) All levers are 'normal' in the frame.

b) A route has now been set for a train to leave the siding and away along the main line. Points 5 have been reversed, followed by the subsidiary ground signal no. 6 and starting signal no. 7. Lock J prevents signal no. 8 from being lowered, whilst lock E prevents the crossover points nos. 4 from being moved. The starting signal no. 7, and the subsidiary signal no. 6 both have to be returned to danger before the points nos. 5 can be reversed again.

33a ▲ 33b ▼

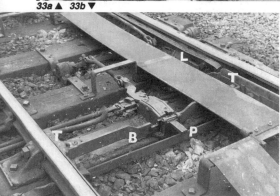

33c ▼

Above, left and below left:
Facing point arrangement,
Bewdley South, Severn Valley
Railway (ex-GWR):
(33a) normal condition showing
the steel plate protecting the lock
mechanism.
(33b) the 'plunger' 'P', passes
through the bar 'B' linking both
the 'toes' (ends of the point
blades) 'T', locking them in
position. Notice that the 'lock
bar' 'L' is low enough for wheel
flanges to pass over it.
(33c) the position of the
mechanism as the facing point
lock lever is reversed in the
signalbox — the 'plunger' is
being withdrawn as the 'lock bar'
reaches the top of the rail. The
'lock bar' cannot be moved if the
wheel of a vehicle is present, and
consequently the point blades
cannot be moved either.

Opposite:
(33d) the facing point lock lever
in the signalbox is fully reversed
so that the 'plunger' is removed
from the bar connecting the toes
of the point.
(33e) the point blades moved to
their new position by the points
lever in the signalbox.
(33f) the 'plunger' passing
through the second notch in the
bar connecting the point blades,
locking them in their new
position. *Author*

3e ▼

being moved. This bolt was in turn connected to a long 'locking bar' which was held in position by the flanges of the wheels of passing trains, thus preventing the facing point lock lever from being operated. *(See photos 33a-f)* In some frames, the 'normal' position of a facing point lock lever was 'reversed'.

At first the normal locking within the lever frame regulated the operation of the relevant point signals depending on the position of the lever in the frame, but eventually as an added protection, the wire connecting the relevant signal to its lever was connected to a bar which passed through the mechanism of the point locks, so that the signal could only be cleared if the point switches and locking had actually functioned correctly. *(See photos 34a&b)* This form of 'detection' was also applied to crossover points, so that the point switches had to be open or closed before the signal could be cleared, and conversely, the point switches could not be physically moved while the controlling signal was still 'off'.

Some companies and signalling contractors also developed 'economical' point locks, most notably the MR, which meant the point switches and the locking mechanism were operated by the same lever.

The Board of Trade's concern about facing

point operation also extended to stipulating the maximum distance they should be from a signalbox. During the 1880s the preferred distance was 150yd which often meant that two or more signalboxes were needed at stations and in goods and marshalling yards. Gradually the distance was relaxed to 200yd at the turn of the century, and 350yd in 1925.

Another important principle in relation to points, was that when the lever controlling them was in its 'normal' position in the frame, the points, where possible, should lie so that they would direct any runaway vehicle away from running lines. If a single point could not achieve this, it became common practice to install 'trap points', ie a point that led nowhere except into the 'fourfoot' (the space between the rails), a stop block or buffer stop, into an earth bank, or just into the 'cess' at the side of the track. For example, where a goods line joined a main line, a trap point would be installed on the goods line just before it began to curve into the main line points. The 'trap' in this location would normally be set so that anything running away towards the main line would be deflected. *(See photo 35)* It was also usual in such a location to connect the point with the trap, so that the two were 'co-acting', operating as if they were a crossover road.

In the 1870s and 1880s, most railway companies bought in their electrical equipment. By the turn of the century most were maintaining, repairing and sometimes modifying instruments, but only the London & North Western Railway had become almost self-sufficient by manufacturing its own designs.

SIGNAL AND LAMP REPEATERS

Originally it was the intention that signalmen should be able to see every semaphore under their control so they could be sure the arm had responded correctly when the lever was pulled. This was obviously not always possible in the case of distant signals (and some stop signals) and so mechanical devices were used to 'repeat' the hidden signal's indication in the signalbox. By 1874 Tyer & Co was marketing an electrical device connected to the semaphore arm which caused a current to flow in opposite directions when the signal was either 'on' or 'off'. The circuit included the familiar pair of coils activating a single-needle unit in the signalbox, with the needle replaced by a miniature semaphore arm to repeat the indication of the real signal. If the signal was neither fully 'on' or 'off', the circuit was broken and the miniature semaphore dropped to a 'WRONG' indication warning the signalman of the problem.

It was also important that a signalman should know whether the lamp of any signal out of sight was lit or not. In 1866, J. A. Warwick had been granted a patent (No 524) for an electrical device to achieve this. His 'lamp repeater' worked on the principle that when a tube of brass inside the signal lamp case was heated by the flame, it expanded and prevented a current running through a circuit to an instrument in the signal station (signalbox). The instrument then indicated 'IN'. When the lamp was not lit, the brass contracted to complete the circuit, moving a flag lettered 'OUT' in front of the 'IN' indication, and ringing a bell in the instrument. In other words the brass tube acted like a switch.

Opposite (36):
The signalman in the ex-North British Railway's Dunbar West signalbox operating the thumb catch of the pegging instrument controlling the down line from Dunbar East, Platform Line. To the right is a non-pegger still retaining its handle for sending dial signals. *G. Ogilvie*

Later, this same simple principle was adopted by others, but in reverse so that it was 'fail safe'. In the lamp case a thin bimetallic strip heated by the flame was kept in contact with another strip thus completing the electrical circuit. When the light was out, the strip cooled, the two pieces of metal parted and broke the circuit, changing the indication in the signalbox repeater to 'OUT'.

By the turn of the century the indications of more and more signals and their associated lamps were electrically repeated in signalboxes.

THREE-WIRE, THREE-POSITION BLOCK INSTRUMENTS

The most common form of block instrument was the single-needle, three-wire, three-position type. Their simple circuitry and function meant all could have been constructed to a standard design, yet it is obvious from the variety of these instruments, that most railway companies ordered equipment to their own particular specifications. For example, in the 1870s the handles of all pegging instruments were held either to the left or right to indicate either 'line clear' or 'train on line', by steel pegs attached to the front of the instruments by brass chains. Twenty years later there were at least three different designs of catch to do the same job — W. E. Langdon's patent catch of 1884 (Patent No 61) used on Midland Railway instruments; J. Radcliffe's patent trigger of 1885 (Patent No 14,954) used on Great Northern Railway instruments; and a neat thumb catch used by the Manchester, Sheffield & Lincolnshire and North British railways on their peggers. *(See photo 36)*

The same variety was to be found with single-stroke bells which, although electrically almost identical, always betrayed their owner's identity in the style of wooden case containing the coils and circuitry. In many signalboxes the variously shaped and highly polished brass domes were proudly displayed on top of the wooden bell cases. In fact so proud of polishing their bells were North Eastern Railway signalmen, that General Rule 66(b) specifically warned them not to remove domes from the instruments in order to clean them. In complete contrast the GNR never had that problem, because the bells used in its signalboxes were rough-cast steel ones hidden away underneath their wooden cases.

In the 1870s the LNWR purchased its block instruments, bells etc from Tyer & Co. Then at the end of 1879 J. W. Fletcher, who like W. Preece and C. E. Spagnoletti, had worked for the Electric Telegraph Co, was appointed the LNWR's Telegraph Superintendent. In 1884 he patented a

combined signal and lamp repeater, and a few years later his son, G. E. Fletcher, also employed by the company, took a number of features from Tyer's one-wire double-needle instruments to develop a two-needle three-wire instrument which included a single-stroke bell and its tapper in the same case. In 1888, within a few months of its appearance, it was adopted as the LNWR's standard block instrument. Various modifications then followed, most notably to the design of the wooden case, and by the turn of the century the 'absolute' and 'permissive' versions achieved their final familiar forms, just over 2ft tall and, due to their monumental appearance, nick-named by some 'tombstone blocks.'

ONE-WIRE, THREE-POSITION BLOCK INSTRUMENTS

As soon as the normal condition of block sections was considered 'closed' and 'line blocked' became a useful third indication (see Part 1 of this chapter), problems arose with two-position instruments. The normal indication on Tyer's needle instruments became not 'line clear' but 'train on line', and with the semaphore variants, the normal position of the miniature arms was raised. Then the 'train on line' indication had to double as 'line blocked.'

Elsewhere the working of Preece and Walker's semaphore instruments was also modified so that the normal indication was with the semaphores raised. Preece's

instruments continued to be used with no attempt to accommodate the third indication, but eventually after Walker's death at the end of 1882, the double plunger device controlling the miniature semaphores of his instruments was replaced by another with one plunger to ring the bell and a disc capable of displaying CLEAR, BLOCKED, and TRAIN IN SECTION.

Spagnoletti's 'disc' instrument suffered in a different way. Because its two indications relied on continuous currents, the disc on the end of the needle could assume a vertical 'line blocked' position, but then half a 'line clear' and half a 'train on line' indication was displayed in the aperture. Despite this drawback, no attempt was made to redesign the disc to show three positive indications even though this was achieved with other similar discs on signal repeaters, further evidence that there was little fundamental new thinking after the 1870s signalling 'revolution.' Spagnoletti's instruments continued in use with this compromised third indication until they were replaced by more modern instruments after World War 2.

Although many companies continued to use two-position instruments long after the advantages of three-position ones had become very obvious, Tyer & Co did begin to redesign its equipment to accommodate a third indication. For the needle instruments used on the Great Eastern Railway, a semi-circular brass flap hinged from two brass brackets, was mounted in front of the two plungers on the main instrument. *(See photo 37)* When its black face was displayed the flap covered the 'line clear' plunger, and a subsidiary flap at its base showed TRAIN PASSED. When 'line clear' was to be given, the flap was turned over the 'train on line' plunger exposing the 'line clear' plunger so that it could be operated, and the flap then displayed its green side and hid the subsidiary flap. When 'train on line' had to be sent, the flap was turned again to expose that plunger, at the same time revealing the subsidiary flap which then displayed TRAIN ON LINE. When the signalman in advance sent 'out of section', the subsidiary flap was turned across the main flap to display TRAIN PASSED again. The flaps were purely mechanical and had no connection with the internal electrical circuitry of the instrument which remained unaltered.

A different mechanical arrangement was tried on instruments used by the Caledonian Railway. When the 'train on line' plunger was depressed to raise the semaphore, a disc to the side of the plunger displayed 'ON' and mechanically locked the 'line clear' plunger. When the signalman in advance sent 'out of section', the signalman in the rear operated a small plunger on the side of the instrument which altered the disc from 'ON' to 'OFF' and released the 'line clear' plunger.

Obviously these two arrangements on the GER and CR relied completely on the integrity of the signalman in control of the instruments, and so Tyer & Co continued to look for an electrical solution to the challenge of providing three indications with one-wire electrics. Once again an existing design was used as the basis. Tyer's instrument which, instead of the two main plungers, incorporated a commutator with integral plunger and screen above, capable of displaying 'line clear' and 'train on line', was adapted to give an additional indication — 'line blocked.' The two-position miniature semaphores were retained, but on instruments supplied to the Glasgow & South Western Railway, for example, at the side of each arm there was an aperture into which a disc appeared showing a blank indication when the semaphore was raised to convey the 'line blocked' or 'normal' indication, and 'ON LINE' when the arm was raised to convey the 'train on line' indication.

Despite these modifications, and the longevity in active service of the instruments mentioned above, any instrument which incorporated miniature semaphores was really obsolete by the 1880s. The first person to devise a one-wire block instrument with needles capable of pointing to three

developed commercially successful one-wire instruments with needles capable of pointing to three separate indications. The firm produced two designs. The first was patented on 1 May 1902, (Patent No 9284) and soon became the standard block instrument of the North Staffordshire and Furness Railways. *(See photo 38)* The sequence of indications was always — 'line clear' — 'train on line' — 'line blocked', which meant that to send 'blocking back' a signalman had to pass the needle through the 'line clear' position first before he could get to 'train on line'. To counteract this deficiency a second mechanism was patented on 8 May 1919, (Patent No 126225) and by some very clever circuitry, indications could be given in any sequence. *(See photo 39)* Instruments incorporating this mechanism were purchased by the London, Brighton & South Coast Railway just before the Grouping and subsequently installed on the main line between Balcombe and Brighton.

PERMISSIVE BLOCK INSTRUMENTS

In May 1879, Edward Tyer was granted a patent, (No 1044) for an instrument with a mechanism which could be used to indicate the number of trains working or standing on the same line at busy stations while maintaining a needle indication at 'train on line'. To display the state of the line and the number of trains, a cylindrical rotatable commutator with integral plunger was incorporated into the instrument. (The commutator was a modification of a device patented in July 1873, (Patent No 1845)). Connected to the commutator inside the instrument was a circular metal disc lettered, LINE CLOSED, LINE CLEAR, TRAIN ON LINE, and Nos 2 to 6. Each of these indications could be displayed in an aperture in the front of the instrument by rotating the commutator. In its three-wire form, the instrument became the standard 'permissive' block instrument of a number of companies. On the LNWR it was at first described as a 'tell-tale' indicator, 'permissive' on that Company's lines still referring to 'time interval' working. The Lancashire & Yorkshire and the Great Central Railways used both this instrument and Tyer's later 'co-operative' permissive instrument, which, as its name implied, needed both signalmen to operate the commutators of their respective instruments simultaneously to alter the indications. *(See photo 40a)*

Not all companies were keen to use these sorts of special instruments, however. For example, where permissive working was in force on Great Northern Railway goods lines, the standard single-needle three-wire block

ndications was Richard Harper. He took his wn existing one-wire instrument design and earranged the circuitry so that the 'line-locked' indication was achieved by eutralising the residual magnetism used to ndicate either 'line clear' or 'train on line'. The atent for this instrument was granted on 6 October 1885, (No 640), but it does not ppear to have been widely used, (if at all) in nis country.

It was not until the beginning of the 0th century, following the standardisation of lock regulations, that Tyer & Co finally

Opposite left (37):
An example of the 'flap' arrangement on Tyer's one-wire two-position needle block instruments used on the Great Eastern Railway. *Author's collection*

Opposite right (38):
A Tyer one-wire three-position needle block instrument (patented in 1902, No 9284) used on the North Staffordshire Railway. *Author's collection*

Above (39):
A Tyer one-wire three-position needle block instrument patented in 1919, No 126225) used on the London, Brighton & South Coast Railway. *Author's collection*

instruments were used, with three indications — 'line blocked', 'line clear' and 'line occupied.'

The Midland Railway used no visual indicating instruments at all when running trains along its goods lines, relying on the exchange of bell codes between signalboxes, and a carefully maintained train register — 'Train Signalling by Telegraph Bells'.

BLOCK SWITCHES

On many lines, traffic was less intensive on Sundays and during the night, and it was therefore not cost effective to keep all signalboxes open all the time. Where signalboxes could be closed occasionally, a 'block switch' or 'closing switch' was provided through which passed all the instrument wiring. By turning a handle on the outside of the block switch, the block instruments in the signalbox could be isolated whilst at the same time creating a circuit connecting the adjacent signalboxes. The procedures for opening and closing signalboxes were contained in Regulation 24.

ROUTE (TRAIN) INDICATORS AND TRAIN DESCRIBERS

As well as block instruments which helped signalmen control the passage of trains between signalboxes, instruments were developed which informed them where a train was going. A number of devices were employed at complex junctions or stations where signalmen controlled a variety of routes and destinations and needed to relay routeing information to their colleagues in advance. The first pair of instruments developed specifically for this purpose were patented by C. V. Walker of the South Eastern Railway in July 1874 (Patent No 1026) and were misleadingly called 'train describers.' They had circular faces and a central needle which could rotate to point to various destinations marked around the circumference. They became very familiar instruments in many busy London suburban signalboxes, where the correct routing of trains was vital through the tangle of lines south of the River Thames.

Walker's instruments were not used by companies north of the Thames, which when they needed 'route indicators' purchased instruments patented by Tyer & Co in December 1879, (Patent No 2575). These had two circular faces with destinations marked around the circumferences. The upper dial incorporated the pointer, whilst the lower one had a central brass disc with holes next to each destination. When a peg was inserted into the appropriate hole the signalman pulled out a spring-loaded plunger on the side of the instrument (in the patent

40a ▲

drawings a lever is indicated). This provided the mechanical power to drive an armature behind the brass disc, in a clockwise direction, making and breaking the electrical circuit as it rotated, and thus moving the pointer on destination by destination. The armature stopped rotating when it reached the peg. In instruments used by the LNWR, the top and bottom dials were marked with the same destinations, the top dial acting as a repeater for the bottom 'transmitting' part. On Great Western instruments, one instrument acted as both sender and receiver, the top dial being activated by the instrument in the adjacent signalbox. *(See photo 40b)* This meant that an instrument used purely for transmitting indications, consisted of just the lower half of a normal instrument, and a receiving instrument was just the upper half.

The LNWR eventually developed its own pair of 'route indicators' in 1891 to the designs of G. E. Fletcher and unlike most other contemporary instruments, they had metal cases. The diameter of the dials varied according to the number of destinations marked around the perimeter.

Not all companies used 'route indicators.' Some relied on telegraphic communication or complex bell codes, whilst others, like the MR, for example, continued to use their block instruments like telegraph instruments. After dial signalling had been abandoned for reinforcing the bell code on receiving 'train on line' — see Part 1 of this chapter — the MR began to issue local routeing dial signal codes. For example, a set of 10 came into use on the main line between South Tottenham Station Junction and Tottenham West Junction on 1 April 1901 and lasted until discontinued by the LMS in 1933 when replaced by a complex set of bell codes.

40b ▼

QUEENS HEAD BOX-RELIEF LINES

Opposite and above (40a&b):
a) Tyer 'co-operative permissive' block instrument.
b) Tyer 'route indicator' from Handsworth & Smethwick signalbox, Great Western Railway. *Author's collection*

ELECTRICAL INTERLOCKING
The weakness of all the block instruments mentioned so far was that they relied completely on the conscientiousness of the signalman operating them. No matter what the block instruments indicated, his signals could be moved completely independently, and having put his signal to 'danger' after the passage of a train, there was nothing to prevent the signalman from immediately pulling the signal to 'clear' again before the train had reached the other end of the section. Equally, there was nothing to stop the indications of block instruments from being altered whilst a train was passing through a block section.

By the turn of the century, the desirability of having the operation of the semaphores connected physically or electrically to the indications of the block instruments was widely appreciated. The two crucial elements were:

1. the locking of the signal controlling entry into a section at 'danger' until the signalman in advance had given a release, (usually 'line clear')

2. the locking of the same signal at 'danger' until the train had passed through the section and the signalman in advance had given 'out of section'.

Systems which accommodated these elements were known as 'lock & block', and by the 1890s there were a number of fully developed types — McKenzie & Holland, Pryce & Ferreira, Saxby & Farmer (Hodgson's Patent), Spagnoletti, W. R. Sykes and Tyer's, with the Midland Railway experimenting with its own system. Of all these, Sykes, and the MR's final form of 'lock & block' were by far the most widely used, and therefore, unlike the others, are worth examining in some detail.

SYKES 'LOCK & BLOCK'
At the beginning of the 1870s William Sykes had been employed in the electrical department of the London, Chatham & Dover Railway, and he had apparently experimented with a 'lock & block' system in 1874 between Shepherds Lane, Brixton and Canterbury Road Junction signalboxes. His first patent was granted on 13 August 1875 (No 662), but it was not until the 1880s that a much improved system was widely adopted on suburban lines south of the Thames. The 1880s type of instrument continued to control lines into the 1960s, the last one being taken out of use in 1984. Nevertheless, even though the operation of the 1875 system and the construction of the instruments were both different from what followed, the principles

were established then and are worth describing here.

Sykes intended that communication between signalmen should be by ordinary single-stroke bell and block instrument, and it is also obvious from the 1875 patent, that he based his system on just home and distant signals. The home signal, of course, controlled entry into the advance block section but contrary to the accepted practice of the day, it was maintained at 'danger' until required to be cleared to allow a train passed. The 'lock & block' instrument which was connected by a rod to the home signal lever, consisted of an upright oblong box with two circular openings above each other. If three signalboxes A, B and C are used as an example, then the normal indication in the lower opening of the instrument at B was a red disc, which covered a fixed white board lettered 'TRAIN FROM A'. The upper opening showed 'CLEAR TO C' on a white disc which covered a fixed board coloured red. This indication was equivalent to 'line clear', the normal position of all block instruments at this date. With the instrument showing these indications, B's home signal would have been locked. Only when it was 'proved' that a train was approaching from A was the semaphore released, achieved when A pulled his signal off to allow the train forward to B. The red disc in the instrument at B then dropped down to reveal 'TRAIN FROM A' in the lower opening, simultaneously sounding a gong, and releasing the lock on B's home signal. When B then pulled his home signal lever, both openings in his instrument showed red, at the same time unlocking the lever in the signalbox at C. When B replaced his semaphore to danger behind the train it became locked again, while the circuitry unlocked the home signal at A. In other words the signalman at A was physically prevented from reversing his home signal lever to allow another train forward to B, until the signalman there had placed his semaphore to danger behind the first train. The same 'proving' of the train through the section continued when C put his home signal to danger behind the train unlocking the home signal at B, and so the procedure was repeated.

By the end of the 1870s, Sykes had improved on the above system, and was granted another patent on 10 November 1880 (No 1907) for an instrument that remained basically unaltered for the next 80 years. The wooden case of the instrument was rectangular with a glazed circular face, behind which there was a screen, into which were cut two rectangular apertures. Behind these apertures two separate flags or 'tablets' could be displayed. The top one indicated either

'LOCKED' or 'CLEAR' (the terminology later changed to 'FREE'), whilst the bottom one indicated either 'TRAIN ON', or 'TRAIN PASSED', 'PASSED' or just blank. Above the wooden case, a miniature semaphore arm with a short brass post, was mounted in a cylindrical tin case with a glass front. *(See photo 41)*

Unlike the 1875 system, the release for the lever lock at B was given by pressing a plunger on the instrument at C. When this release was given, 'TRAIN ON' was displayed in the lower aperture of C's instrument, whilst at the same time the miniature semaphore on the instrument at B changed from the clear to the danger position, and 'CLEAR' (or later 'FREE') appeared in B's upper aperture. The signalman at B could then pull off the signal controlling entry into the section. Once the signal was pulled off, the upper aperture displayed 'LOCKED'. A treadle was also introduced into the system, placed just beyond the section signal, which when the last vehicle of the train had passed clear of it,

released the lock on the lever controlling that signal, changing the upper aperture display from 'LOCKED' to 'CLEAR', (later 'FREE'), allowing the signalman to place the semaphore to 'danger'. Once at 'danger', the lever was once again locked, with 'LOCKED' displayed in the upper aperture. When the train arrived at C and the signalman there replaced his semaphore to 'danger' behind it,

Opposite (41):
Sykes 'Lock & Block' instrument.
Author's collection

Above (42):
The interior of East Dulwich signalbox, London, Brighton & South Coast Railway. The Sykes 'Lock & Block' instrument with the plunger nearest the camera, shows TRAIN ON, indicating that the Dulwich signalman has pressed the plunger and accepted an up train from Knights Hill. The 'plunging' instrument also shows that the up home signal, No 2, is FREE, while the adjacent instrument with the top miniature semaphore indicates that the up starting signal (the section signal) No 3 is locked, and therefore the signalman has not yet received a release from the signalman at Peckham Rye. The down line signals, Nos 23–25) have been pulled off at the far end of the frame for a train going forward to Knights Hill.
National Railway Museum; 483/2/68

the lower aperture in his instrument changed from 'TRAIN ON' to 'TRAIN PASSED', 'CLEAR' or blank, and at the same time lowered the miniature semaphore arm in B's instrument, indicating that the line was once again clear.

At some point Sykes also developed a double semaphore instrument obviously based on C. V. Walker's design, intended to work in conjunction with his 'lock & block' device without the top semaphore indicator. In the circular face of this second instrument there were two miniature semaphore arms, and on the back of the case a single-stroke bell. At the bottom of the case was the bell tapper and at the side of it a commutator for raising or lowering the right-hand semaphore arm. In 'open' block working, when a signalman wanted to send a train forward through a block section, he would tap out the appropriate code on the tapper, and if the signalman in advance could accept it, as well as pressing the plunger on the 'lock & block' instrument, he would also turn his commutator to raise both his right-hand miniature semaphore and the left-hand semaphore in the instrument at the signalbox in rear. Once the train had arrived safely, the miniature semaphore could be lowered again. When 'closed' block working was introduced, the miniature semaphore was normally kept in the 'danger' position.

Building on the 1880 patent, Sykes soon added a 'switch hook' to the main 'lock &

block' instrument which was used to turn over the plunger. When the train entered the section and the appropriate bell code was sent to the signalman in advance, that signalman turned this switch hook over the plunger on his instrument. If the system incorporated miniature semaphores above the main instruments, turning the switch hook raised the arm to 'danger' at the sending end. If Sykes double semaphore instruments were employed, as well as turning the switch hook across the plunger on the 'lock & block' instrument, the signalman also turned the commutator on his double semaphore instrument which then raised the left-hand semaphore arm in the instrument at the sending end.

In relation to 'closed' block working, it is interesting that until the 1960s and 1970s, the top semaphore indicators on instruments controlling ex-London, Brighton & South Coast and South Eastern & Chatham lines were normally in the 'clear' position, ie open block, compared with those on ex-London & South Western lines which were normally at 'danger', ie closed block. (NB The Southern Railway used the terminology 'open' and 'closed' differently to this historical interpretation, in a way that is explained in Chapter 6.)

Sykes 'lock & block' was installed on most of the suburban lines south of the River Thames, as well as on the Hull & Barnsley Railway when that opened in July 1885 and the Lancashire, Derbyshire & East Coast Railway when it opened in December 1896. On these lines where home and starting signals were used, two instruments controlled each line. The plunging instrument contained the lock for the home signal, its normal condition being FREE until the arm had been lowered, after which it remained locked until the train had passed it. The other instrument, without the plunger, and referred to by the northern companies as the 'electrical instrument', contained the lock for the starting signal, normally locked until a release (a plunge) had been given by the signalman in advance. This instrument also carried above it the miniature semaphore arm. *(See photo 42)* Both the H&BR and the LD&ECR operated 'open block' sections, with the miniature semaphore normally lowered to indicate that the section was unoccupied. A version with a three-position needle indication in place of the top semaphore was also used by the North British Railway.

The final refinement to the system allowed the section signal to be put to 'danger' in cases of emergency before the train had passed over the treadle and released the lock. In these circumstances, the lever was not restored fully to its normal position in the frame, but just far enough to allow the semaphore arm to return to the 'danger' position without releasing the interlocking in the lever frame.

In 1896 probably the most sophisticated version of Sykes 'lock & block' was installed on the Great Eastern Railway out of London. Basically the instruments operated as described above, but with an additional indication of TRAIN ACCEPTED as well as TRAIN ON. But that was not the only change. The Achilles heel of previous Sykes instruments had been the release key. This could be used in two ways: 1. to raise the TRAIN ON indication and thus release the lock on the plunger if it had to be pressed a second time to unlock the signalbox in rear's section signal, and 2. if the section signal had been pulled 'off' but the train had been cancelled before passing over the releasing treadle, the key had to be used to unlock the lever so that it could be put back fully into the frame. The GER system was so contrived that in the first case the signalman in the rear had to press a button to electrically unlock a shutter across the release keyhole in the advanced instrument. While the shutter was open and the key in the instrument, the circuit between the two signalboxes was broken, removing any risk of the signalman leaving the release key permanently in the instrument. In the second case, the signalman in advance had to press a button to electrically release the 'back-lock' on the rear signalbox's section signal. Co-operation in this way reduced the risk of abuse.

THE MR'S 'ROTARY INTERLOCKING BLOCK' INSTRUMENT

Sykes 'lock & block' was a clever system, but during the years when it was being perfected, other engineers had been trying to develop much simpler electrical systems based around the familiar single-needle block instrument. For example, W. E. Langdon, who as an employee of the Midland Railway, had developed his own 'lock & block' system by the 1890s based on that Company's existing three-wire pegging block instrument. His experiments were carried forward by others and finally led to the perfection of a unique system. Given the MR's rejection of all other specialist instruments, this development is all the more interesting. The company could have used Sykes equipment as installed on the GER, for example, but J. Sayers, the MR's telegraph engineer considered this '...suitable only for suburban and through running traffic...'.

Looking at what the MR finally adopted, it is obvious that an important consideration was to reduce as far as possible the differences between any new 'lock & block' system and what already existed. The resultant 'lock & block' instrument was, therefore, simply a replacement for a standard three-position single-needle 'pegging' instrument. The receiving 'non-pegging' instrument remained electrically unaltered except for the addition of a 'line clear' release button, in fact many old instruments were refurbished for their new role. Ordinary single-stroke bells were used in the traditional way to communicate between signalboxes, and therefore, standard block procedures remained unaltered, and under normal operating conditions, signalmen did not have to modify their working practices. The new system was first tried out at the beginning of 1909, and after various modifications and improvements, was finally patented on 1 April 1915 (No 9134).

The new 'pegging' instrument had the standard three-position, single-needle unit, mounted in a wooden case of approximately the same proportions as a standard instrument. However, the feature which distinguished it from the ordinary instruments and which gave rise to its name, was the 4½in diameter brass disc with its central short bakelite handle which rotated through a full 360° replacing the normal drop handle. Behind the brass disc, the mechanism and circuitry were all designed around this rotary motion giving rise to the official name — 'Rotary Interlocking Block.' *(See photo 43)*

The normal 'line blocked' position of the handle was vertical. When the handle was rotated clockwise by 120° to indicate 'line clear', this released (lifted) the lock on the signal controlling entry into the section from the rear, allowing the signalman there to pull the signal 'off.' As with the Sykes arrangement, the signalman only had 'one pull', and once the pull had begun, he could not replace the lever until it had been fully reversed. When the signalman in rear transmitted the 'train on line' bell code to the signalbox in advance, the signalman there moved the handle clockwise through another 120°. This operation had three important consequences.

1. the lock on the 'section signal' would fall so that this signal, once returned to 'danger' after the train, could not be pulled again until the full sequence of block indications had been completed and another 'line clear' had been received.

2. the handle on the instrument remained locked in the 'train on line' position until that signalman's home signal had been pulled 'off' to allow the train past, then returned to 'danger' and, more importantly, until the train

had passed completely over a treadle just 'inside' that home signal. Once all that had been achieved, the signalman could send the 'train out of section' signal and turn the handle another 120° clockwise to the 'line blocked' (normal) position.

This was the usual sequence of events, but as with all sequential instruments connected electrically to the operation of signals and train-activated treadles, there had to be built-in cancelling and resetting devices. In the 'rotary' system there were three release buttons. On the 'pegging' and 'non-pegging' instruments there was a 'line clear' cancelling

Above (43):
A Midland Railway 'Rotary Interlocking Block' instrument.
Author's collection

button. The co-operation of both signalmen was required to create an electrical circuit to lift the mechanical lock of the handle so that it could be turned anti-clockwise back to the 'line blocked' (normal) position. The second release was for cancelling 'train on line.' It was purely mechanical and only on the 'pegging' instrument, but as the button was behind a thin piece of glass which once broken had to be replaced by the lineman who had to insert a printed and signed release card, its use was effectively monitored. In later instruments, the mechanism and electrics were modified so that 'train on line' could be indicated for 'blocking back' purposes, without having to use the 'train on line' cancelling button.

In addition, at junctions the circuitry could be arranged so that facing point locks had to be in their correct positions before a 'line clear' could be given, and once that had been sent, those locks could not be altered until the train had passed over the releasing treadle. (See photo 44)

The 'pegging' rotary instrument was also fitted with a tapper just beneath the handle, which could be moved from side to side to send routeing signals when the handle was vertical, either in the 'line blocked' (normal) position, or exactly between 'line clear' and 'train on line'. After dial signals had been abandoned in 1933, the tappers were gradually removed.

Above (44):
Cambridge Street signalbox, ex-Midland Railway, showing the frame and block instruments which controlled the lines to and from St Pancras Junction signalbox. All but one of the single-needle movements has a green dial lettered 'Midland Railway.' The plastic lever numbers are a London, Midland & Scottish Railway addition. Notice that although No 13 is a working lever, it has no number plate! *BR (London Midland Region)*

TRACK CIRCUITS

Eventually, treadles were replaced by track circuit control, the final, and in relation to modern signalling practice, probably the most important development of traditional signalling.

The principle of the track circuit is that a train will automatically announce its presence to a signalman independently of any fixed signals or manually operated block instruments. This is achieved by isolating stretches of track and incorporating both sets of rails into a circuit running through a relay. The current keeps the relay in operation. When a train stands on that stretch of track, its wheels create a short-circuit, isolating the relay, which then completes another circuit which can either alter the indication of a single-needle unit in the signalbox, (a track circuit indicator), or illuminate a light in the track diagram. All track circuit indicators based around single-needle units were constructed so that they would 'fail safe', ie if the circuit failed, gravity caused the disc, banner, needle, etc to indicate 'line occupied.'

The principle of the track circuit and the way it could be implemented electrically, had been known about in the 1870s, but the equipment was not reliable enough until much later. By the turn of the century, more use was being made of track circuits, but their widespread use on ordinary main lines did not happen until after a tragic accident on the MR. On 24 December 1910, the overworked signalman at Hawes Junction forgot he had two light engines standing at his down-advanced starting signal. The fireman of one of the two engines should have walked to the signalbox and reminded him of their presence according to Rule 55, but failed to do this. The signalman having been offered a down express, gave the signalman in rear a 'line clear', and then obtained a 'line clear' himself from the signalbox in advance, and pulled off for the express. Once he cleared his starter, the light engines started away unknown to the signalman, followed a few minutes later by the express. One and a half miles from Hawes Junction it ran into the back of the two engines.

There were three ways this accident could have been avoided, only one available to the signalman at the time. If one of the firemen had carried out Rule 55 correctly, he should have visited the signalbox and signed the train register. On some companies it was then standard practice for the signalman to place a 'lever collar' over the top of the home signal lever preventing the catch handle from being operated. When something out of the ordinary was taking place, the use of a lever collar in this way acted as a physical reminder to a signalman who might otherwise operate signal levers instinctively.

The two other safeguards not available to the Hawes Junction signalman both depended on track circuiting. Firstly, if a track circuit had been installed immediately in rear of the starting signal, operating an indicator in the signalbox, the signalman would have been reminded of the presence of the light engines. The second, and more useful use of the track circuit in this situation, would have been to link it with the 'pegging' instrument. When the light engines were standing at Hawes Junction's starter, the block indications were correctly at 'line blocked' (normal) and there was nothing to stop the signalman giving a 'line clear' to the signalman in the rear. However, if the light engines had been standing on a track circuit, the circuitry could have been arranged so that a 'line clear' could not have been given, and consequently the section signal of the signalbox in the rear would have remained locked.

This is precisely what was implemented in subsequent 'rotary interlocking block' installations. By the end of 1913, as a direct result of the Hawes Junction accident, the MR had installed 374 lengths of track circuiting, and 379 rotary interlocking block instruments, and by the Grouping of 1923, a significant proportion of the company's main lines were protected in this way.

TELEPHONE
Finally, mention must be made of the telephone. This device began to find its way into signalboxes in the 1890s, and was an important element in the creation of centralised control systems on railways like the MR and the L&YR. Although the telephone proved invaluable, providing communication between signalbox and station, between marshalling yard staff and signalmen, and eventually for communicating between footplate crew at signals and signalmen, it was not normally used for the exchange of block signalling information except on some goods lines and when block bells and/or instruments failed. It never completely supplanted the 'speaking' telegraph instrument either until after steam had disappeared from the railway network. In busy signalboxes the telephone tended to restrict a signalman's movements. It was always a great advantage to be able to listen to the telegraph whilst pulling levers and answering block bells. The final working telegraph instruments lingered on in service on the former GNR main line, for example, until the early 1970s.

PART 4: SINGLE LINE CONTROL

As outlined in Chapter 2, because single lines were inherently more dangerous than double lines, they were some of the first to be controlled by the electric telegraph. Tyer & Co soon developed a one-wire device based on its standard double-semaphore instrument modified with a flap which alternately covered the 'Signal On' (equivalent to the 'train on line') plunger, and the 'Signal Off' (equivalent to 'line clear') plunger. This instrument appeared in the firm's 1874 catalogue. By the 1870s, a number of single lines were controlled by the 'Absolute Block' system.

But the employment of the ordinary single-needle telegraph or Tyer's device, of course, did not remove the possibility of instrument misuse or misunderstanding, and some companies took a more physical approach to controlling traffic. This could involve the use of an engine to pilot all trains through the single line section, or in place of the engine, a special 'pilotman' to ride on the train engine. Both these methods could be costly and time-consuming, and consequently some companies began to replace the pilot or pilotman with a wooden staff, which footplate crews had to be in possession of before they could pass through the section. The use of 'staff' working was strongly advocated by the Board of Trade in the 1860s.

However, even the use of pilots or staffs had their drawbacks. In theory trains had to pass through the section alternately from either end. As this was obviously not always possible, if more than one train had to leave one end of the section before another returned from the other end, the first train would be dispatched after having been merely shown the staff, which then followed on the last train travelling in the same direction. Eventually, to confirm that a driver had been allowed into a single line section after having been shown the staff, drivers were issued with a ticket, obtained from a box unlocked by a key set into the end of the staff.

The use of 'staff & ticket' in combination with the telegraph became the normal operating practice on single lines (and survived into the 1960s), but following a head-on collision between Thorpe and Brundall on the Great Eastern Railway in September 1874, Edward Tyer devised a system which combined the advantages of both telegraphic communication and staff working. A pair of instruments and two forms of circular 'tablets' (or discs as they were called in the patent) just over 4in in diameter were patented on 24 May 1878, (Patent No 1262). Two instruments were placed at either end of a single line section, one containing a number of tablets for issuing to train crews, the other for receiving tablets issued at the other end of the section. The tablets replaced the single staff, and 'up' and 'down' line tablets differed slightly so that they could not be passed through the wrong instrument. As with ordinary block working using Tyer's equipment, the signalmen communicated with each other by pressing plungers which activated bells or gongs. A commutator and plunger on the receiving instrument, released the lock on the issuing instrument at the opposite end of the section. Once a tablet had been freed from the issuing instrument, another could not be obtained from either end of the section until the first had been passed through the receiving instrument. This action then released the lock on the issuing instrument so that another tablet could be obtained from either end of the section.

The advantage of this system was that as

TYER & CO. LIMITED.   NO. 6 TABLET INSTRUMENT.   LONDON & CARLISLE

DIAGRAM OF CIRCUITS

there were a number of tablets available in the issuing instruments, more than one train could be dispatched safely from one end of a section, and whereas tickets were only substitutes for the real staff, each train in Tyer's system carried the full authority of a tablet.

The disadvantage, however, with different tablets for 'up' and 'down' trains, was that periodically tablets had to be removed from the receiving instrument and taken from one end of the section to the other to be placed back in the issuing instrument. As only one tablet could be released at a time, it became

obvious that separate 'up' and 'down' line tablets were unnecessary and could be replaced with only one type for the section. As long as the tablets for adjacent sections were different and could not be passed through the wrong instrument, there was no danger and both the issuing and receiving instruments could be combined.

Edward Tyer developed these ideas and within a few years had modified his original instruments and devised a standard form of tablet. Each tablet had engraved on its face the names of the signalboxes at either end of the section, and more importantly had a small notch cut into the side, the shape of which differed for every section, so that tablets could only be inserted into the appropriate instruments for the section they controlled.

Despite the advantages of the system, it appears that the Railway Inspectors of the Board of Trade took some time to recommend its use. In 1884 when the Great North of Scotland Railway was about to extend its single line, the Board of Trade tried unsuccessfully to persuade it to use staff working with Absolute Block. The compromise was the installation of the tablet system. Clement E. Stretton's Safe Railway Working, does not mention the tablet system at all. Nevertheless, Tyer & Co continued to refine its tablet equipment, and on the 9 November 1888, Edward Tyer was granted a patent (No 42) for an improved instrument, the No 6, which became one of his most successful single line products. (See photo 45)

Still, not every company opted to use Tyer's equipment, no doubt partly due to the Board of Trade's reluctance to recommend the tablet system, and in that same year A. M. Thompson and F. W. Webb of the LNWR took out a joint patent for their own single line device. By the 1880s the LNWR was manufacturing almost all its own signalling equipment, and although realising the obvious advantages of Tyer's system over its own 'staff & ticket' operation, it was averse to buying from outside contractors. It also sought continuity with its existing system and therefore developed an Electric Train Staff instrument. 'Instrument' is perhaps not the best description for the robust cast iron machine that resulted from the joint patent.

Opposite (45):
Tyer & Co's No 6 Tablet Instrument.
Author's collection

Left (46):
Webb & Thompson's single line electric staff instrument. This particular example lacks the usual right-hand indicator and bell tapper. Ian Allan Library

The final form of the equipment which evolved after minor modifications, stood 3ft 6in tall and was capable of storing 18 metal staffs. *(See photo 46)* The disposition of the rings along the shaft of the staffs varied for each section so they could only be placed into the relevant pair of machines, one at either end of the section.

Interestingly, Edward Tyer considered the LNWR device infringed his patent, and successfully made the LNWR pay a royalty of £2 per machine. A few years later in 1892 he developed and patented his own electric staff instrument, (Patent No 18,603) but it never became as popular as the Webb & Thompson equipment which, made under licence by the Railway Signal Co, was used by a number of railway companies. A miniature version was available from 1906.

Tyer's tablet and Webb & Thompson's electric staff systems continued in use until nationalisation and beyond, but by then the most widely-used system was 'key token' working. This had been patented in 1912 by Blackall the Signal Engineer of the GWR and his assistant Jacobs. The Marlow branch was the first to receive the new equipment at the beginning of 1914, and Tyer & Co was granted the licence to manufacture and market it. The instrument became No 9 in the firm's range of single line equipment and it gradually replaced Webb & Thompson's Electric Train Staff on all GWR single lines. It then became and remained the standard on all Britain's railways until the late 1980s and is still used on preserved lines like the Severn Valley Railway.

In the No 9 instrument, the tablet had in effect evolved into a key, while the instrument had become the equivalent of an oversized door lock. When the key token was locked in the instrument, its end stuck out like an ordinary key, with the name of the section it controlled visible on the end. The only difference in comparison with an ordinary door lock was that the instrument could contain a number of identical keys.

At the top of the instrument's metal case, there was a centrally-pivoted single needle, (the galvanometer), and, just below it, the hole where the key token was inserted and extracted. To the right of the keyhole was the plunger. The signalmen exchanged bell codes on this plunger, which deflected the single needle on each stroke. After the exchange, the signalman accepting the train kept the plunger depressed for a few seconds, which lifted the lock to allow the other signalman to extract the token. To achieve this, the token had to be brought up to the keyhole and turned anti-clockwise through 180°, as though the signalman was unlocking an ordinary door lock, except that the turn involved two distinct movements. The first broke the circuit between the two instruments causing the single needle to drop to the vertical position, and the second re-established it, the resulting flicker of the needle indicating to the receiving signalman that the token had been successfully extracted. The signalman then turned a pointer to the left of the keyhole to indicate that a token had been removed. If there was a level crossing between the signalboxes, this action could be used to bring a single needle into circuit there to indicate that a train was approaching. On later instruments the mechanical pointer was replaced by a single-needle unit, which indicated whether a token had been released from that

Below (47):
Tyer & Co's No 9 single line key token instrument inside Pickburn signalbox. A key token has been inserted into the keyhole. *R. Pratley*

Opposite (48):
The fireman of GWR-design No 7821 Ditcheat Manor on a Saturdays-Only Birmingham–Pwllheli train in August 1965, about to give up the key token from Hookagate on leaving Westbury, Shropshire. In the background the post carrying the hoop and key token for the next section to Buttington Crossing can just be seen. *John R. P. Hunt*

instrument or from the other end of the section, the wording being — LINE NORMAL, TRAIN COMING FROM, TRAIN GOING TO. *(See photo 47)* When the key token was returned to the instrument, it was turned clockwise in the keyhole, as if locking it in.

Once out of the instrument, the tablet or token was placed in a leather pouch attached to a metal hoop so that it could be caught by the fireman of the passing train. Some staffs were also attached to hoops, but usually they were considered large enough to hand directly to the fireman on the footplate. At passing places, where speeds were low and trains were either slowing to stop or just departing, the hoops could be dispatched and caught by signalmen and fireman comparatively easily. *(See photo 48)* If speeds rose, however, this practice was no longer safe, and therefore a number of special catchers and dispatchers were designed for the lineside and the side of the locomotive or its tender. On predominantly single-track railways like the Midland & Great Northern, the Highland and the Somerset & Dorset, the use of exchange equipment was vital to maintain an effective service.

Where sidings on single lines were too far away to be controlled directly from signalboxes, a key built into the end of a staff, the staff itself, or a tablet could be inserted directly into a ground frame to unlock its levers, or into an instrument for controlling that ground frame which would give an electrical release. Similar ground frames were used on double lines to control remote sidings, the usual form of release for many years being an 'Annetts key', a device patented by J. E. Annett of the London Brighton & South Coast Railway in October 1875. The key would be issued from the nearest signalbox, and when removed would lock signals and/or points in that signalbox until it was returned.

RULES & REGULATIONS
Almost all the standard Rules & Regulations could be and were applied to single line working using tablets, staffs or key tokens, with a number of important additions:

1. If a train was double-headed, the tablet, staff or key token was always carried in the cab of the train engine. If an engine was assisting a train in the rear, then the tablet, staff or key token was carried by that engine.

2. The criteria for clearing points remained the same for single lines with the addition that at designated crossing places, 'line clear' could be given if the facing points were correctly set for the approaching train and the line was clear to the starting signal whether it

was a quarter of a mile in advance of the home signal or not. If both lines at crossing places were clear to the starters, and the points set correctly, trains could be accepted from either direction. If both trains arrived at the same time, both had to be brought to a stand at the home signals, before one of the trains was allowed forward to the starting signal. Once this train had come to a stand within the loop, complete with tail lamp, the home signal for the other train could be lowered to allow that forward.

3. Normal 'blocking back' procedures applied to single lines with the relaxation that if a train was travelling away from a signalbox, a train could follow it into the section for shunting purposes only without sending 'blocking back' to the signalman in advance. However, if shunting was still taking place when 'out of section' was received from the signalman in advance, the 'blocking back' signal (3 pause 3) had to be transmitted. In Regulation 7 of token working, additional protection for shunting outside the home signal could be provided for by the withdrawal of a token — (5 pause 2).

SINGLE LINE WORKING ON DOUBLE LINES
Single line working on double lines was always a temporary expedient when engineering work or some other obstruction closed one line. This form of working was not normally considered an emergency, but the Rules were framed as if it was. As with true emergencies, every eventuality had to be considered and procedures rigourously implemented if the problems were not to become more dangerous. Only an outline of procedures can be given here.

To accompany each train through the affected section between signalboxes, a pilotman would be appointed. To distinguish his role, he had to wear a red armband with white lettering on his left arm above the elbow. 'Single Line Working Forms' had to be completed by all staff involved, and until everyone had signed those forms, no train was allowed through the section. If more than one train had to pass in one direction, the pilotman would issue the driver with another written form which he had to surrender to the signalman at the far end of the section. The pilotman would then travel on the footplate of the following train. Where trailing points became facing points, the blades had to be held in the correct position by padlocked metal clips. If possible, block working would be maintained, and once the obstruction had been removed, but before normal working could begin again, the pilotman would collect all the forms issued.

Traditional signalling reached its zenith at the beginning of the 20th century. By then, mechanical interlocking and block working had been perfected, and the conscientious adherence to Rules & Regulations meant Britain's railways had an enviable safety record. The largest mechanical lever frames ever constructed date from this period: Cannon Street No 1 opened April 1893 with 243 levers; Edinburgh Waverley East opened July 1898 with 260 levers; and the largest of all, York Locomotive Yard opened in June 1905 with 295 levers. *(See photo 49)*

In reality, mechanical interlocking could be developed no further, and the huge lever frames like those mentioned above were at the limits of mechanical efficiency as well as at the limits of signalmen's physical stamina and endurance to operate. *(See photos 50 & 51)* The way ahead was with the increasing use of pneumatic and ultimately electrical power to operate points and signals so that miniature lever frames, and eventually signalling panels, could reduce the size of signalboxes, reduce maintenance and by default reduce the physical labour of the signalman.

Below (49):
Severn Bridge Junction signalbox at Shrewsbury, built by the LNWR at the turn of the 20th century, and equipped with 180 levers. *John Titlow*

But signalling, and the way it was carried out, as with all facets of railway operation, reflected a wider social ethic, and throughout British society at the turn of the century, there was a belief in permanence and stability. There were managers and engineers prepared to fundamentally rethink accepted practices, but on the whole management thinking was dominated by a belief in very cautious progress, and while labour remained a comparatively cheap commodity in the railway budget, there was little incentive to change the status quo.

Following World War 1, however, with a reduction in signalmen's hours and a significant rise in wages, combined with growing evidence that theoretical electrical engineering could achieve more in practice than traditional methods of signalling, there were incentives for change. New ideas and new devices like colour light signalling, track circuiting and route setting, automatic signalling and train control, tried to a limited extent before the war, were developed after the conflict, and through the 1930s began to lay the foundations for modern signalling practices. The interwar years witnessed a revolution in signalling as important as that of the 1870s.

Despite the potential of all the new technology, however, apart from track circuiting which became increasingly important on all main lines, fundamentally

new developments remained almost completely self-contained in isolated locations, and apart from on the Southern Railway, they did not challenge existing operating practices to any extent until well after World War 2. Many of the elements of traditional mechanical signalling were refined and improved, but the basic principles remained unaltered. As a result, the majority of the country's network of lines continued to be controlled by the block system with semaphore signals worked by mechanical lever frames until the 1960s, and consequently, of the new developments after the turn of the century, only those which augmented traditional signalling will be considered here.

LEVER FRAMES

Once railway companies had conformed to the requirements of the 1889 Act, and instigated absolute block working on all passenger lines, and completed the interlocking of all connections with running lines, there was a significant fall in demand for new mechanical signalling equipment. Signalling contractors found it increasingly difficult to keep their businesses going, and in 1901 all the major firms except Stevens & Sons and Tyer & Co came together under a new holding company, the Pneumatic Electric & General Engineering Co Ltd, later renamed the Consolidated Signal Co Ltd. Manufacturing capacity and the range of products was reduced, and in 1920 the firms within the holding company were taken over by the Westinghouse Brake & Saxby Signal Co. Tyer & Co and the Railway Signalling Co

Top (50):
Point rodding at the base of Kidderminster Town station signalbox, Severn Valley Railway, 1994. *Author*

Above (51):
Signal wires at Kidderminster Town station, Severn Valley Railway, 1994. *Author*

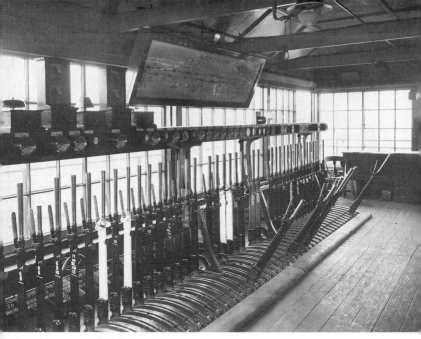

Above (52):
The McKenzie & Holland lever frame in ex-North Eastern Railway signalbox, Boothferry Road in the mid 1930s. On the block shelf are two of the LNER 'standard' double line block instruments with their associated single-stroke bells. Along the front of the shelf are single-needle signal repeaters. *Ellison Hawks*

continued to trade separately, and Stevens & Sons, which had ceased to trade in England in 1916, finally went out of business when its works in Scotland closed in 1923.

There was still a need for new lever frames, but the post-Grouping railway companies made more use of reclaimed mechanical equipment, making up lever frames from secondhand parts. This, combined with the variety of equipment on lines absorbed in 1923, precluded complete standardisation. In 1921, the Railway Executive Committee had recommended that all companies adopt an updated version of the Midland Railway frame, but in practice these new 'REC' frames only found their way into the signalboxes of those companies absorbed into the LMS. The new frames were made by the LMS at both Crewe and Derby until the signal works at the latter closed in 1932. Crewe continued to manufacture and eventually under British Railways management, produced the final version of the MR family of frames designed during World War 2 — the London Midland Region Standard.

Saxby & Farmer's 1914 patent (No 4873), with slight modifications, became the Westinghouse group's standard mechanical frame, (the A2), in 1924. It was used by the LNER and was designated the SR's standard at the end of the 1920s. McKenzie &

Holland's Nos 16 & 17 designs had become the standard on the Southern Division of the North Eastern Railway before World War 1, and then were used by the LNER and BR(NE) all over former NER territory until the mid-1960s. *(See photo 52)* In Scotland, the LNER continued to install Stevens pattern frames made by the Railway Signal Co even though that firm's development of the last Great Central Railway frame was officially designated the LNER's standard. Examples of the latter were confined to the Southern Area of the system. Where new mechanical frames were needed in Scotland after nationalisation, the Westinghouse A3 frame, a variant of the A2, became the preferred choice.

Needless to say, the Great Western Railway and its successor the Western Region of BR continued to manufacture its own distinctive frame and install it new until the mid-1960s, and secondhand until 1981. Produced just after the Grouping, the Vertical Tappet 5 Bar, was undoubtedly a fitting conclusion to the evolution of the mechanical lever frame. Somehow, no matter what one's company loyalties, the GWR's last designs culminating in the Vertical Tappet 5 Bar, seem to epitomise what the ordinary railway enthusiast would expect of the typical lever frame.

By the Grouping, there was general agreement between railway companies as to the colours levers should be painted.

Stop signals, including subsidiary signals	red
Stop signal released by 'line clear'	red with horizontal white stripe
Distant signals	green (gradually yellow was substituted)
Intermediate Block Signals	red (top) yellow (bottom)
Points	black
Facing point locks	blue
Facing points with combined locks	blue & black
Gate locks	brown
Detonator placers	black & white chevrons, pointing upwards for 'up' lines, and down for 'down' lines
Spare — non-operational	white

SEMAPHORES

Having disappeared from Britain's railways by the beginning of the 1880s, the three-position semaphore signal reappeared in a modified form during World War 1 when the South Eastern & Chatham Railway imported a number of American upper quadrant examples and erected them at Victoria station, London. The arms displayed 'danger' when at 90° to the post; 'caution' when at 45° inclined upwards; and 'all clear' when vertical and parallel with the post. These three positions dispensed with the need for separate stop and distant signals. A driver encountering an arm at 'all clear', knew the next signal would be at either 'all clear' or 'caution', and if at 'caution' knew the next signal would be at 'danger'. In this way the driver always had advanced warning of a 'danger' indication which was obeyed as any conventional home or starting signal.

After the War the Great Western, Great Northern and Great Central Railways, began to make limited use of these upper quadrant three-position semaphores, and at the Grouping it seemed likely that such signals would become a common sight on Britain's railways. However, following the recommendations of the Three Position Signal Committee of the Institution of Railway Signal Engineers at the end of 1924, all the major companies except the GWR agreed to work towards three and four-aspect colour light signalling for future main line work, and where traditional semaphore signals were preferred, to develop and install two-position upper quadrants — both stop and distant — as a new standard.

The advantage of the upper quadrant was that it did not need a heavy spectacle casting and push rod from the base of the signal post to be fail safe. As with many lower quadrant signals, the new upper quadrant semaphores were made in two parts, the spectacle fabrication being common to both stop and distant signals. The separate arms were at first made of corrugated steel sheet, the preferred material of the LNWR since 1883, and painted the appropriate colours. Later the arms were formed from a flat sheet turned up at the top and bottom edges and enamelled. (See photo 53) Smaller versions of both the spectacle and arms were manufactured for sidings, and a miniature red arm with a central horizontal white stripe was made for 'calling-on' purposes.

Gradually throughout the 1930s these new standard semaphores began to appear on the lines of all the major companies except the GWR, which developed its own improved version of lower quadrant also with an enamelled arm. (See photo 54) On the LNER and SR, new upper quadrants often simply replaced lower quadrants on existing posts. (See photo 55) The LMS did the same but also developed tubular posts, new standard brackets and gantries which were used extensively all over the country after nationalisation.

Above left (53):
Standard upper quadrant home and distant semaphores with enamelled steel arms at Lincoln Central, 1990. Notice the curved plates behind the arms to obscure the 'back light' from the lamps when the semaphores are in the 'off' position. *Author*

Left (54):
Standard Great Western Railway, British Railways (Western Region), lower quadrant home signals with 'calling-on' arms beneath, at Kidderminster Town, Severn Valley Railway, 1994. *Author*

Above right (55):
Co-acting semaphores at Selby North in June 1950 with standard upper quadrant arms above and ex-North Eastern Railway lower quadrant arms pivoted in slots in the posts beneath. *G. Oates*

The standardisation of ground signals proved more difficult to achieve. During the 1930s hundreds of pre-Grouping examples were still in use, and although there was agreement that the indications of all new ground signals should be made by circular discs with a white ground and horizontal red band, the form of the mechanism used to operate them still varied between companies.

Finally mention must be made specifically of distant signals. The change to a yellow aspect during the 1920s helped footplate crews enormously in identifying these signals, but in the next decade as the speed and consequently braking distances of expresses increased, the reaction of drivers to them became ever more crucial. Improvements, however, were slow to materialise. One was to move traditional semaphores further away from the home signals, but more effective was the erection of colour light signals instead. The latter became increasingly familiar on main lines still controlled by semaphore stop signals and the block system. When a colour light signal was operated from a mechanical frame, because the lever became in effect just an electrical switch and needed little effort to operate, the top would be cut down by a few inches to remind the signalman not to exert too much force. (The same applied to any lever which activated a point motor or electrical release.) The final improvement, pioneered by the GWR and only used to any extent by that company before nationalisation, was to give drivers an audible indication of the distant signal's aspect which would also automatically begin a brake application, if the arm was showing caution. The GWR's Automatic Train Control (ATC) was eventually superseded by the British Railway's Automatic Warning System (AWS).

TRACK CIRCUITING AND BLOCK CONTROL

By the 1930s, track circuiting had progressed beyond merely indicating in the signalbox the presence of a train on a certain section of track. The accepted aim between the wars was to combine track circuiting with block control, to compel signalmen to carry out block signalling in the correct sequence, as with the MR's 'Rotary Interlocking Block'. This was not because signalmen were less reliable than before, but because just one slip when running faster trains and heavier rolling stock could be disastrous.

This was unfortunately and dramatically demonstrated on the night of 15 June 1935, when the LNER signalman at Welwyn South pegged another 'line clear' before the preceding train had cleared the section resulting in that train being hit in the rear by an express running at nearly 70mph. The accident occurred only three months before the *Silver Jubilee's* record-breaking inaugural run. On 27 September, that train raced past

the scene of the accident at 98mph, and attained 112mph only 17 miles further north at Arlesey.

The Inspecting Officer recommended that in future the track circuiting should be so arranged that a train had to prove that it had passed through the section, ('proving' in railway terminology), and the full sequence of block indications completed with all the signals cleared and returned to 'danger', before another 'line clear' could be given.

In this period, 'berth' track circuits were already being installed in rear of the outermost home signal, (the first stop signal an approaching train would encounter), to ensure that when that track circuit was occupied it maintained the indication on the block instrument at 'train on line'. The refinement after Welwyn was to extend this protection so that once a 'line clear' had been transmitted, the train had to clear both the berth track circuit and the block section before another 'line clear' could be given. To reinforce this protection at locations where a starting signal was provided, a second track circuit was installed on the approach side of that signal. This berth track circuit operated in exactly the same way as the other, but then both had to be cleared in the correct sequence, and the signals returned to 'danger' after the passage of the train before the block instrument could be unpegged, 'train out of section' sent, and another 'line clear' given to the signalman in rear. These arrangements of block and berth track circuit control, became known as 'Welwyn control'.

As with any 'lock & block' system, however, arrangements had to be made so that 'line clear' could be cancelled, and if the home or starting signal lever had been pulled, it could be replaced before a train had passed the signal. In the former case, the electrical release was obtained by rotating the handle on a small device, next to the pegging instrument, for just over a minute. In the latter, the lever could be returned far enough in the frame to place the semaphore arm to 'danger' but not far enough to free the frames

Opposite (56):
Friars Junction signalbox, Great Western Railway in 1931. Track circuits are indicated in the illuminated diagram. Below the diagram on the shelf are four 'combined' Spagnoletti block instruments with associated single-stroke bells, and to the right three permissive block instruments made to Edward Tyer's 1879 patent, No 1044. Hanging on the block shelf are four lever collars.
Real Photos, no 25131

interlocking. The electric lock then held the lever in the intermediate position for 2min before it could be returned fully to the normal position in the frame. The time involved in gaining either a block or signal lever release, gave the signalman enough pause for thought to consider his actions.

Where any track circuits were operative on the approach side of signals, it also became the standard practice to attach to the signal post a white diamond approximately a foot across indicating to train crews that Rule 55 did not apply, except if they were detained at the signal for an unusually long time. Signals protected by 'Lock & Block' equipment also carried the same diamond sign.

As the 1930s progressed, most track circuits in main line signalboxes were indicated, not by separate instruments on the block shelf but, in the actual layout diagram above the block shelf and lever frame. *(See photo 56)* The track circuits were indicated by small electric bulbs placed in the appropriate tracks on the diagram. When the tracks were occupied, the lamps were illuminated, and when clear, the bulbs were extinguished. All the major companies developed 'illuminated diagrams', but needless to say, each used its own standards, so that BR inherited at least four different systems.

The increasing use of track circuits and block control also led to the replacement of many mechanical clearance bars, locking bars and treadles, and when frames had to be relocked as layouts changed, more of the interlocking was achieved electrically.

INTERMEDIATE BLOCK SIGNALS
Another advantage to be gained from extending track circuiting, was the abolition of signalboxes whose function was simply to break otherwise long block sections. Hundreds of these 'break section' signalboxes, many with no more than four levers to control up and down line home and distant signals, had been constructed by the Victorians.

An early 20th century solution was to install automatic or semi-automatic semaphore signals, operated either pneumatically or electrically by the passage of a train. The best known installation was along the LSWR's main line between Woking and Basingstoke, (1902). The NER's main line between Thirsk and Alne was also equipped with automatic and semi-automatic electro-gas signals at almost the same time (1903-4).

The trend between the wars, however, was to use ordinary home and distant semaphore signals driven by electric motors but controlled from the signalbox in rear of them. The first experimental installation of these

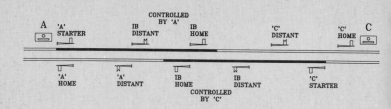

CONTROLLED
BY 'A'

A   'A'   IB   IB   'C'   'C'   C
     STARTER   DISTANT   HOME   DISTANT   HOME
                   M   M

     'A'   'A'   IB   IB   'C'
     HOME   DISTANT   HOME   DISTANT   STARTER
                                   CONTROLLED
                                   BY 'C'

Fig. 7

'advance section' signals had been on the GWR main line at Basildon near Goring in 1907. Once the signals were found to work well in practice, other sets were installed elsewhere on the system.

Other railway companies followed the GWR's lead, the new 'intermediate block' (IB) signals allowing them to abolish a number of break-section signalboxes. The position of those signalboxes' home and distant signals was retained, but their control was transferred to the signalboxes either side of them. *(See Fig 7)* Track circuits extended from the signalbox in rear to a quarter of a mile beyond the IB home. The signalman sending the train forward needed no 'line clear' to pull his ordinary signals off but required a 'line clear' from the signalbox in advance to be able to clear the IB signals. Usually the IB home and distant signals were operated from one lever painted red and yellow. The usual practice was to send 'train on line' as normal when the train passed the signalbox, but as the IB home was in reality the section signal, the GWR logically instructed its signalmen to send 'train on line' when the train passed that signal. A bell or buzzer sounded in the signalbox when the train passed the IB home signal. The signalman would not be able to clear his ordinary signals again for a following train, until the first train had cleared the track circuit in advance of the IB home, and the lever controlling that signal had been restored

to the normal position in the frame. In early installations the IB signals were returned to 'danger' by this lever, but it became usual, especially where colour light signals were substituted for semaphores just before, and then as a matter of course after World War 2, for the signals to return to 'danger' automatically after the passage of a train. *(See photo 57)* As with any track circuit installation, the progress of the train was indicated either by separate instruments or on the illuminated diagram in the signalbox. If a

Opposite (57):
Ex-Great Central signalbox, Barnetby East, in 1989. In the foreground the levers controlling the up fast line have been pulled 'off'. No 18 controls the colour light distant signal; Nos 19 & 20 the home signals; No 21 the starter and No 22 the Intermediate Block home and distant signals. Connected to the home, starter and IB levers just above floor level are the electrical track circuit and line clear release locks, whilst above them are the 'economiser contact' locks for the starter and IB levers. By lifting the catch-handle when the lever is 'normal' in the frame, the economiser contact energises the lock so that track circuit and line clear release circuits can be 'proved'. *Author*

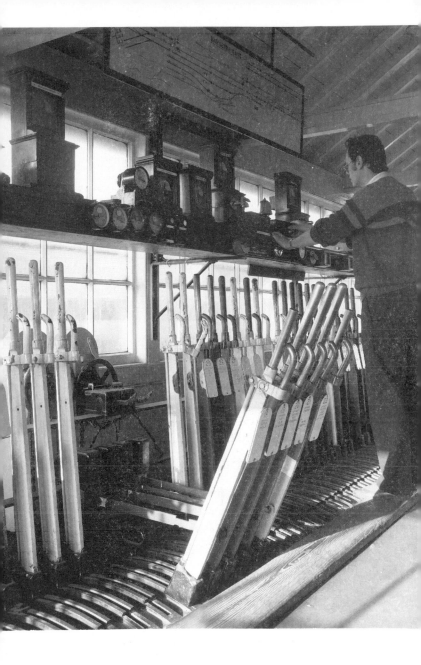

train passed an IB signal at 'danger', the bell or buzzer sounded continuously to alert the signalman.

IB signals created in effect two block sections in any one direction. This meant that a signalman could legitimately pull his ordinary signals off, allow a train forward, return those signals to 'danger' behind it, see that train steam away into the distance and accept another train in rear, before obtaining a 'line clear' in advance for the IB signals. To traditional signalmen this must have been initially slightly unnerving.

STANDARD BLOCK INSTRUMENTS

Despite their drawbacks, Tyer's one-wire block instruments were probably the neatest of all early designs, having both up and down line indicators in one case, and the single-stroke bell/gong with its plunger or tapper all mounted together on one piece of timber. The firm's three-wire instruments were even more compact, although they did not incorporate a single-stroke bell, and they could also be mounted on conventional block shelves above the lever frame. By the turn of the century, Tyer & Co had modified its one-wire designs, so they too could be fitted onto a block shelf. Two versions of this instrument became the new standard for the Caledonian and Glasgow & South Western Railways.

In other three-wire systems, the usual arrangement was to have separate pegging and non-pegging instruments and bells, but at the turn of the century there was a trend towards combining these separate pieces of equipment. The LNWR had instruments incorporating all the above components in one case by the 1890s — see Chapter 5, Part 3. The GWR heightened the case of its standard Spagnoletti instrument so as to incorporate the non-pegging indication, but did not go as far as to include the bell and its tapper. The L&YR produced its own design of three-wire block instrument which incorporated both up and down line single-needle indicators, and a bell plunger integral with the commutator. The single-stroke bell, however, remained a separate item. The GNR produced a limited number of its own combined instruments, but they seem to have been used in only a few locations. The designs also varied, but those in use around London and Spalding were constructed out of a standard single-needle pegging instrument case with the addition of a suspended bell at the top, and a commutator working a mechanical 'line clear'/'line blocked'/'train on line' indicator with a bell tapper to its right.

These various attempts at rationalisation, unfortunately only added to the great variety of block instruments inherited by the new companies at the Grouping of the railways in 1923. At this time the Rules & Regulations Committee of the RCH recommended that for double lines, three-position, three-wire block instruments should become the standard. All railway companies tried to a greater or lesser

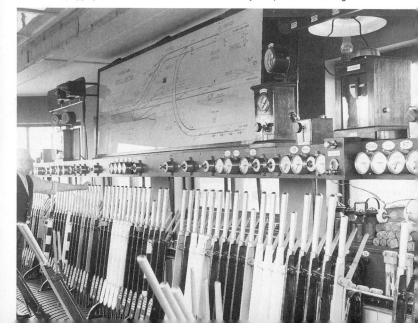

extent to rationalise their equipment and replace one-wire with three-wire instruments, but by nationalisation in 1948, many instruments dating back to the 1870s and 1880s, including hundreds of one-wire varieties, were still in use all over the country.

Of all the Grouping companies the SR probably inherited the biggest selection of instruments, and therefore it is not surprising that it was the first to design and introduce a standard three-position block instrument. As an example of the antiquity of equipment still in use when the SR was formed, the very last pair of Preece miniature semaphores manufactured to the original 1862 Patent and therefore not incorporated into a case, were taken out of use from Southampton Junction and Yard signalboxes as late as 1927.

The new SR instruments resembled Sykes 'lock & block' equipment, and were in use by the end of the 1920s. (See photo 58) As they began to appear, 'open' and 'closed' block working took on new meanings. In 'closed' working, the block instruments were linked electrically with both track circuits and lever locks, to provide the electrical equivalent of 'lock & block' working:

1) the signal controlling entry into a block section was locked until a 'line clear' had been given by the signalbox in advance.
2) both the distant and home signal (or outer home if provided) had to be in the 'on' position before a 'line clear' could be

Opposite (58):
The Westinghouse 'A2' lever frame in Strood Junction signalbox, Southern Railway, June 1939. Nearest the camera on the right is a Walker's one-wire, two-position double semaphore block instrument controlling the lines to and from Wickham Siding. To the left is a Southern Railway standard three-wire, three-position block instrument controlling the lines to and from Chatham Goods Sidings.
Real Photos, No 24947

Above (59):
A pair of standard Great Western Railway, British Railways (Western Region) block instruments and block switch inside Shirley signalbox, 1981.
W. H. A. Thompson & D. J. Powell Collection

given — 'block proving'.
3) stop signals had to be proved to be at 'danger' and then pulled off in sequence, in the order in which an approaching train would encounter them — 'signal proving' and 'sequential locking'.

In 'open' block working, usually confined to branch lines, apart from the second element, there were no electrical links between the block instrument and levers although there might be track circuits.

The only other Grouping company to design a new standard block instrument before nationalisation was the GWR. The first sets were installed experimentally in Reading West Junction and Reading Main Line West signalboxes in November 1947 and then at Scours Lane, Tilehurst and Pangbourne just before Christmas that year. The new instruments gradually replaced Spagnoletti's equipment throughout the 1950s and remain the standard instrument on former Western Region lines at the time of writing. *(See photo 59)*

Other companies' attempts at rationalisation often involved more than one 'standard' instrument. For example, the LMS continued to use the LNWR's design of block instrument, but also purchased Tyer & Co's new Type F design of combined instrument for use in Scotland. The LNER also purchased a number of new designs from signalling contractors, and for use in the North Eastern Area, modified existing single-needle instruments to create a new standard. That instrument incorporated two-needle units and a commutator with cylindrical knob. The single-stroke bell with its tapper remained a separate item. At a later stage the original form of commutator was replaced by a rotary design, similar but not identical to the MR version, and this was also added to ordinary single-needle pegging instruments when the original peg and chain was removed.

The same commutator was incorporated into a double-line three-wire instrument manufactured by Tyer & Co, (smaller than the Type F), and this was another new design purchased by the LNER. The instrument incorporated the bell tapper and had the single-stroke bell mounted on the back of the case. In this form it resembled another new instrument manufactured by R. E. Thompson & Co and used to a limited extent by the LNER on the former GNR main line. As with the hybrid GNR instruments, the bell on the Thompson instrument was mounted above the case.

It was some time before BR introduced what was to become *the* standard form of block instrument to replace many of the instruments mentioned so far, a piece of equipment which is still considered as today's standard wherever block working remains in force. The very neat design was prepared under the supervision of S. Williams, Signal Engineer of the London Midland Region, and was proudly described in the Railway Gazette for November 1956. The new instrument was based on two basic plastic modules of the same dimensions, capable of being connected and stacked on top of each other. One module could be adapted to incorporate

either a single-stroke bell and its tapper, or the single-needle indicator, while the other module housed the commutator, in either an absolute or permissive form. Instead of the usual induced needle, the armature was a permanent magnet actuated by a single coil. To control a normal double line, the new standard instrument would be assembled from four modules — bell and tapper, commutator, and two needle units. *(See photo 60)*

CONCLUSION

The decade in which steam-hauled trains stopped running in this country also witnessed a drastic reduction in the amount of freight travelling by rail. Sidings, marshalling yards and hundreds of miles of track were lifted or abandoned. There was far less shunting to be carried out, far fewer trains to deal with, and consequently far less lever pulling for signalmen to do. The detailed Rules & Regulations which had evolved to cope with unpredictable loose-coupled steam-hauled goods trains, and intensive passenger services, were seen as increasingly restrictive. One by one the main lines were resignalled with multi-aspect colour light signals controlled from 'power boxes' or 'signalling centres' and now, at the end of the 20th century, traditional signalling, with just a few exceptions, is confined to branch lines and preserved railways. It is almost impossible to believe that according to W.M. Acworth in his 'Railways of England' published in 1900, 900 to 1000 levers were worked per hour in Waterloo 'A' signalbox, which meant that every signalman moved a lever every 15 seconds.

No museum or preservation group can fully recreate or evoke the heyday of traditional mechanical signalling, At the time of writing (1994), in the author's opinion, the following were amongst the best places to gain a convincing impression of what was once commonplace:

1. The Severn Valley Railway is traditionally signalled throughout with lower quadrant semaphores of Great Western Railway and British Railways (Western Region) origin.

2. Exeter West signalbox was built by the Great Western Railway in 1912 and in 1959 was fitted with a 131-lever, Vertical Tappet 5 Bar frame. The signalbox was rescued by the Exeter West Group in 1985 and re-erected at Crewe Railway Heritage Centre complete with its frame and instrumentation.

3. The Midland Railway Trust at Butterley and Swanwick operates a single-track line with authentic Midland Railway equipment most of which can be seen at close quarters.

The last standard set of RCH Rules printed before World War 2 appeared in 1933, with various amendments being issued just before the conflict. The next revised edition appeared in 1950 to become the first BR standard Rule Book. Many of the Rules, particularly in relation to the use of flags and hand lamps during shunting operations, could be traced back to the Rule books of the 1840s.

The first standard BR Regulations for Train Signalling were issued by the RCH on 1 October 1960, followed during the next few years by numerous amendments. These took the form of sheets of tear-off slips which signalmen had to paste by one edge into their original volumes. Both these sets of Rules and Regulations, and their amendments, probably the most comprehensive ever issued, served the railways until the end of steam.

Rules & Regulations, however, formed only a small part of the mass of paperwork that signalmen had to make themselves familiar with. Railway companies had printed Working Timetables for the use of operating staff since the 1850s. By the 1950s these were comprehensive documents produced by every Region and invariably issued as separate booklets for individual locations or lines. They listed, amongst other things, almost every train movement with departure, passing, waiting, and arrival times. In addition, signalmen would receive separate notification of special trains and how they were to be dealt with.

Working Timetables were supported by volumes of Sectional Appendices listing all signalboxes, their opening times, relief lines, distances between signalboxes, speed restrictions and detailed local arrangements such as whistle codes, siding capacities, etc.

Periodically, Operating Areas within Regions would issue notices of signalling alterations and circulate these to operating staff. The notices would warn train crews and signalmen of the position of new signals, the abolition of signalboxes, temporary speed restrictions and the dates of engineering work, etc.

In addition, signalmen had to know all the Special Instructions appertaining to their particular signalbox. These instructions would include notes on whether certain Regulations did or did not apply at their signalbox, list special bell codes, and record the position of the 'fogging point' and who to contact to call out the Fogmen.

Then there was a plethora of smaller booklets, advising staff on the working of Royal Trains, or on what abbreviations were current for the sending of telegrams or telegraph messages, as well as sheets of Wrong Line Order Forms, Fogging Tickets, Block Restoration Tickets etc, etc.

Below (60):
British Railway's modular standard double-line absolute block instrument.
Author's collection

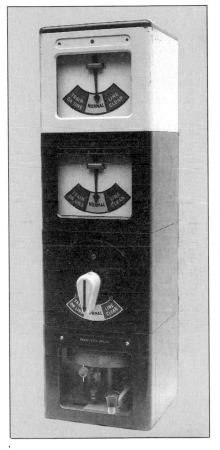

REGULATIONS

The following were the first standardised regulations for the signalling of trains on double track by the Absolute Block System with ordinary block instruments on the Eastern, London Midland, North Eastern, Scottish and Southern Regions of British Railways, published in *Regulations for Train Signalling and Signalmen's General Instructions* by the Railway Clearing House on 1 October 1960. Because of limited space, the explanatory texts accompanying certain Regulations have been omitted, as have the special Regulations for Permissive and Single Line Working.

ABSOLUTE BLOCK SYSTEM			
BELL SIGNALS			
See Regula-tion	**Class of train**	**Description**	**Code**
APPLICABLE TO ALL REGIONS			
	-	Call Attention	1
APPLICABLE TO ALL REGIONS EXCEPT SOUTHERN			
1 & 4	A	Is line clear for:- Express passenger train, newspaper train, breakdown van train or snow plough going to clear the line, or light engine going to assist disabled train Officers' Special train not requiring to stop in section Electric express passenger train	4 consec-utively 4-2
	B	Ordinary passenger train, mixed train, or breakdown van train NOT going to clear line Electric ordinary passenger train Branch passenger train (Where authorised)	3-1 3-1-2 1-3
	C	Parcels, fish, fruit, horse, live-stock, meat, milk, pigeon or perishable train composed entirely of vehicles conforming to coaching stock requirements Express freight, livestock, perish-able or ballast train, pipe fitted throughout with the automatic brake operative on not less than half of the vehicles	1-3-1 3-1-1

See Regulation	Class of train	Description	Code
		Empty coaching stock train (not specially authorised to carry 'A' headcode)	2-2-1
		Electric empty coaching stock train	2-2-1-2
	D	Express freight, livestock, perishable or ballast train, partly fitted with the automatic brake operative on not less than one third of the vehicles	5 consecutively
	E	Express freight, livestock, perishable or ballast train, partly fitted, with not less than four braked vehicles next to the engine and connected by the automatic brake pipe Express freight, livestock, perishable or ballast train, with a limited load of vehicles NOT fitted with the automatic brake	1-2-2
	F	Express freight, livestock, perishable or ballast train, NOT fitted with the automatic brake	3-2
	G	Light engine or light engines coupled (See Regulation 3)	2-3
		Engine with not more than two brake vans	1 1 3
	H	Through freight or ballast train, not running under class 'C', 'D', 'E' or 'F' headcode	1-4
	J	Mineral or empty wagon train	4-1
	K	Freight, mineral or ballast train, stopping at intermediate stations	3 consecutively
		Branch freight train (Where authorised)	1-2
1,5 & 8	K	Freight, ballast or Officers' Special train, requiring to stop in section	2-2-3
1,5 & 9		Trolley requiring to go into or pass through tunnel	2-1-2
1		Train entering section	2 consecutively

See Regula-tion	Class of train	Description		Code
APPLICABLE TO THE SOUTHERN REGION ONLY				
1 & 4		Is line clear for:- PASSENGER TRAIN OR BREAKDOWN VAN TRAIN OR SNOW PLOUGH NOT GOING TO CLEAR THE	MAIN LINE	3-1
			BRANCH LINE	1-3
		BREAKDOWN VAN TRAIN OR SNOW PLOUGH GOING TO CLEAR THE LINE OR LIGHT ENGINE GOING TO ASSIST DISABLED TRAIN	MAIN LINE	2-2
			BRANCH	4-4
		FISH, MEAT, FRUIT, HORSE, CATTLE, MILK OR PERISHABLE TRAIN COMPOSED OF COACH-ING STOCK	MAIN LINE	4-2-2
			BRANCH	2-2-4
		EMPTY TRAIN	MAIN LINE	2-2-1
			BRANCH	1-2-2
		FREIGHT OR THROUGH BALLAST TRAIN	MAIN LINE	3-2
			BRANCH	2-3
		LIGHT ENGINE OR LIGHT ENGINES COUPLED (See Regulation 3)	MAIN LINE	4-1
			BRANCH	1-4
		ENGINE WITH NOT MORE THAN TWO BRAKE VANS	MAIN LINE	3-1-1
			BRANCH	1-1-3
1,5 & 8		FREIGHT, BALLAST OR OFFICERS' SPECIAL TRAIN REQUIRING TO STOP IN SECTION		5 consecutively
1,5 & 9		TROLLEY REQUIRING TO GO INTO OR PASS THROUGH TUNNEL		2-2-2
1 & 5 (ALSO SIGNAL-MEN'S GENERAL INSTRUC-TIONS)		POWER-WORKED INSPEC-TION CAR OR MECHANI-CALLY OR POWER-WORKED TROLLEY	THROUGH	2-3-2
			REQUIRED TO STOP IN SECTION	1-3-1
1		TRAIN ENTERING SECTION	MAIN LINE	2 consecutively
			BRANCH	4 consecutively
10		ENGINE ASSISTING IN REAR OF TRAIN		1-4-1

See Regula-tion	Class of train	Description	Code
		ENGINE WITH ONE OR TWO BRAKE VANS ASSISTING IN REAR OF TRAIN	1-5-1
APPLICABLE TO ALL REGIONS			
1 & 4 (Also Out-of-Gauge Instruc-tions)		Train which can pass an out-of-gauge or exceptional load similarly signalled on the opposite or an adjoining line	2-6-1
		Train which cannot be allowed to pass an out-of-gauge load of any descrip-tion on the opposite or an adjoining line between specified points	2-6-2
		Train which requires the opposite or an adjoining line to be blocked between specified points	2-6-3
		Opposite line, or an adjoining line used in the same or opposite direction to be blocked for passage of train conveying out-of-gauge load	1-2-6
1		Train approaching (where authorised)	1-2-1
2		Cancelling	3-5
		Last train signalled incorrectly described	5-3
5		Warning Acceptance	3-5-5
		Line now clear in accordance with Regulation 4 for train to approach	3-3-5
6 & 12		Train out of section, or Obstruction removed	2-1
7		Blocking back inside home signal	2-4
		Blocking back outside home signal	3-3
		Train or vehicles at a stand	3-3-4
APPLICABLE TO ALL REGIONS EXCEPT SOUTHERN			
10		Engine assisting in rear of train	2-2
		Engine with one or two brake vans assisting in rear of train	2-3-1
APPLICABLE TO ALL REGIONS			
11		Engine arrived	2-1-3

See Regula- tion	Class of train	Description	Code
11		Train drawn back clear of section	3-2-3
12		Obstruction Danger	6 consecutively
16		Train an unusually long time in section	6-2
17 & 20		Stop and examine train	7 consec- utively
19		Train passed without tail lamp	9 consec- utively to box in ad- vance; 4-5 to box in rear
20		Train divided	5-5
21		Shunt train for following train to pass	1-5-5
22		Train or vehicles running away in wrong direction	2-5-5
23		Train or vehicles running away in right direction	4-5-5
24		Opening of signalbox	5-5-5
		Closing of signalbox	7-5-5
		Closing of signalbox where section signal is locked by the block	5-5-7
26		Testing block indicators and bells	16 consecutively
31		Shunting into forward section	3-3-2
		Shunt withdrawn	8 consec- utively
32		Working in wrong direction	2-3-3
		Train clear of section	5-2
		Train withdrawn	2-5
Signal- men's General Instruc- tions		Distant signal defective	8-2
		Home signal defective	2-8

CALL ATTENTION

Except in the case of the following bell signals, and as otherwise provided in Regulation 12(f), the *Call Attention* signal must always be sent before any other signal and must be acknowledged immediately on receipt:-

Train entering section.
Train approaching (where authorised).
Warning acceptance.
Engine assisting in rear of train.
Engine with one or two brake vans assisting
 in rear of train
Obstruction Danger

NOTE.- On the Southern Region the *Call Attention* signal will not be used preceding the *Train out of section* or *Obstruction Removed* signals.

REPETITION AND ACKNOWLEDGMENT OF SIGNALS

Except as provided for in Regulations 5, 8, 9 and 12(f), all signals must be acknowledged by repetition and no signal must be considered as understood until it has been correctly repeated to the signalbox from which it was received. When the *Is line clear* signal is not acknowledged, it must be sent again at short intervals.

REGULATIONS

1. MODE OF SIGNALLING

'A', 'B' and 'C' represent three consecutive signalboxes, and the process of signalling a train is as follows:-

(a) Prior to the despatch of a train from 'A' the Signalman there, provided he has received the *Train out of section* signal for the previous train and the block indicator is in the normal position, must call the attention of 'B', and having obtained it, send the proper *Is line clear signal*. If the line is clear at 'B' the Signalman there may acknowledge the signal and place the block indicator to the *Line clear* position.

(b) The Signalman at 'A' may then, if the line is clear, lower his signals for the train to leave 'A'.

(c) On the train leaving 'A' the Signalman there must send the *Train entering section* signal to 'B', and the Signalman at 'B' must acknowledge the signal and place the block indicator to the *Train on line* position.

(d) 'B' must then, provided he has received the *Train out of section* signal for the previous train, and the block indicator is in the normal position, call the attention of 'C', and having obtained it, must send the proper *Is line clear* signal to 'C'. On receiving permission from 'C' for the train to approach, 'B' may lower his signals for the train to proceed to 'C', and when the train has arrived at or passed 'B' or has been shunted clear of the line at 'B', the Signalman there must call the attention of 'A' and, having obtained it, send the *Train out of section* signal, which signal must be acknowledged, and place or maintain the block indicator at the normal position.

(e) Where special authority has been given in order to avoid delay to the train, the *Is line clear* signal must be sent forward as soon as the *Is line clear* signal has been acknowledged and before the *Train entering section* signal has been received from the box in rear, when this can be done in accordance with the Regulations under which the *Is line clear* signal may be sent.

(f) Where it is necessary that a Signalman who has acknowledged the *Is line clear* signal for a train should receive an intimation of its approach before it enters the section, the *Train approaching* signal (1-2-1) must, where authorised, be sent in accordance with the special instructions issued.

NOTE.- On the Southern Region the *Call attention* signal will not be used preceding the *Train out of section* signal.

2(A). CANCELLING SIGNAL (3-5)

2(B). LAST TRAIN SIGNALLED INCORRECTLY DESCRIBED (5-3)

3. ENGINES AND ENGINES AND BRAKE VAN COUPLED TOGETHER

4. LINE CLEAR OR GIVING PERMISSION FOR A TRAIN TO APPROACH

(a) Except where instructions are issued to the contrary, the line must not be considered clear, nor must a train be allowed to approach from the box in rear in accordance with Regulation 1, unless the line, or at a junction the line for which the facing points are set, is clear for at least a quarter of a mile ahead of the home signal, and all the necessary points within this distance have been placed in their proper position for the safety of the approaching train subject to the provisions of clause (f) of this Regulation.

Where the outermost home signal is situated at least a quarter of a mile in rear of the next home signal a train must not be allowed to approach from the box in the rear unless the line is clear to the latter signal and any points between these signals have been placed in their proper position for the safety of the approaching train.

(b) Where the outermost home signal of the box is less than a quarter of a mile from the outermost home signal of the box in advance, the Signalman at the former box must not give permission for a train to approach from the box in rear until *Train out of section* or the *Train out of section* bell signal has been received from the advance box, or, when the 3-3 signal has been acknowledged to the advance box, until the *Obstruction Removed* signal has been received or the obstruction has been transferred from outside to inside the home signal in accordance with Regulation 7(B)(e).

In the event of failure of the block apparatus between two boxes where the outermost home signal for the rear box is less than a quarter of a mile from the outermost home signal of the advance box and trains are being worked in accordance with Regulation 25(a)(iv), the Signalman at the former box must not accept a train from the box in rear in accordance with this Regulation until it has been ascertained that the line is clear to the outermost home signal for the box in advance. If this cannot be done, the train may be accepted in accordance with Regulation 5, provided the line is clear as far as can be seen and all points have been placed in their proper position for the safety of the approaching train, the Signalman at the box from which the train is to be accepted being previously advised of the circumstances.

(c) After a train has been accepted in accordance with this Regulation no obstruction of the line on which the train requires to run, or of the line for which the facing points at a junction are set, must be allowed within a distance of a quarter of a mile ahead of the home signal or other prescribed clearing point, except as provided in Regulation 14(d), until —

    (i) the train has been brought to a stand at the home signal, or

    (ii) the train has passed beyond any connections within

    the clearing point which may require to be used, or

    (iii) the *Cancelling* signal has been received for the train concerned.

(d) If the line is not clear or if from any other cause the Signalman is not in a position to give permission for the train to approach when the Signalman in rear sends the *Is line clear* signal, that signal must not be acknowledged until the Signalman to whom the signal has been sent is prepared to accept the train.

(e) During fog or falling snow —

(i) except where instructions to the contrary are issued or as shown in Regulation 14(b), if a Fogsignalman is not on duty at the distant signal, the *Is line clear* signal must not be acknowledged in accordance with this Regulation unless the line under the control of the Signalman requiring to acknowledge the signal is clear, all the necessary points have been placed in their proper position for the safety of the approaching train, the *Train out of section* signal or *Obstruction Removed* signal has been received from the box in advance, and the block indicator worked from that box, is in the normal position. In addition, where the distance from the box to the outermost home signal of the box in advance is less that half a mile, the *Is line clear* signal must have been acknowledged by the latter box.

When a train has been accepted in accordance with the first sentence of the preceding paragraph, a *Blocking Back* signal must not be acknowledged to the box in advance until the train concerned has been brought to a stand at the home signal, or the *Cancelling* signal has been received. Similar conditions apply in connection with the last sentence of the following paragraph.

Where the outermost home signal is situated at least a quarter of a mile in rear of the next home signal, the *Is line clear* signal must not be acknowledged in accordance with this Regulation when the line is clear only to the latter home signal unless Fogsignalmen are on duty at the distant signal and at the outermost home signal; if, however, a Fogsignalman is on duty at the distant signal only, the *Is line clear* signal may be acknowledged in accordance with this Regulation provided the line is clear for a least a quarter of a mile ahead of the home signal next in advance of the outermost home signal. If the outermost home signal for the box in advance is within that distance a train must not be accepted unless the *Train out of section* signal has been received for the previous train and the block indicator is in the normal position.

(ii) in the event of failure of the block apparatus between two boxes and trains are being worked in accordance with Regulation 25(a)(iv), the Signalman at the rear box must, when no Fogsignalman is on duty at the distant signal, accept trains in accordance with Regulation 5 provided the line is clear in accordance with clause (a) of this Regulation (4) and the Signalman at the box from which the train is to be accepted has been previously advised of the circumstances.

(iii) except where instructions are issued to the contrary, unless a Fogsignalman is on duty at the distant signal, permission must not be given in accordance with this Regulation for a passenger train to approach from the box in rear with the facing points set for a direction where it is necessary that speed should be reduced, unless it is the route booked in the publications headed 'Working Time Table' or 'Supplement to Working Time Tables', but the train must be allowed to approach in accordance with Regulation 5, provided the line for which the facing points are set is clear in accordance with this clause (e).

(iv) except where instructions are issued to the contrary, Fogsignalmen will not be employed at colour light signals. Such signals may be regarded as if Fogsignalmen were stationed at them.

(f) AT JUNCTIONS, except where a home signal is provided at least a quarter of a mile in rear of the junction home signal [and subject to the provisions of clause (e)], the approach of trains, which can cross or foul each other, must be regulated as shown below:-

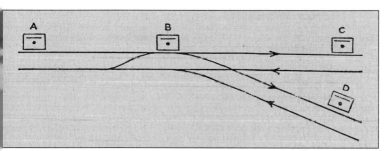

(i) When permission has been given by 'B' for a train to approach from 'C', no train must be allowed to leave 'D' until that from 'C' has been brought to a stand at the junction home signal or has passed a quarter of a mile beyond the junction home signal applicable to a train coming from 'D', or if the home signal at 'A' is within that distance, until the line is clear in accordance with clause (b) of this Regulation; nor in such a case must a train be allowed to leave 'A' for 'D' unless the junction facing points at 'B' are set for 'C' and the line towards 'C' is clear in accordance with clause (a) or (b) of this Regulation, as applicable.

(ii) When permission has been given by 'B' for a train to approach from 'D', no train must be allowed to leave 'C' until that from 'D' has been brought to a stand at the junction home signal, or has passed a point a quarter of a mile beyond the junction home signal applicable to a train coming from 'C', or if the home signal at 'A' is within that distance, until the line is clear in accordance with clause (b) of this Regulation.

(iii) When permission has been given by 'B' for a train to approach from 'A' for 'D', no train must be allowed to leave 'C' until that from 'A' has been brought to a stand at the junction home signal or has passed clear of the junction or the junction facing points have been set for 'C' and the line towards 'C' is clear in accordance with clause (a) or (b) of this Regulation, as applicable.

(iv) When a train at 'B' has been sent towards the starting signal for the direction of 'C' or 'D' and the rear of the train is well clear of the junction, permission for a following train to approach from 'A' may be given if the points are set for the other line, and that line is clear in accordance with clause (a) or (b) of this Regulation, as applicable.

(v) Where an additional home signal is situated at least a quarter of a mile in rear of the junction home signal, the additional home signal must not be lowered for a train to proceed towards the junction home signal if a conflicting movement has been authorised or a train accepted in accordance with this Regulation from another direction in which there is no such additional home signal, until the movement which has been authorised has passed clear of the junction or the train which has been accepted from another direction has been brought to a stand at the junction home signal or has passed clear of the junction. When, however, a train for which the additional home signal has been lowered has come to a stand at the junction home signal, a movement may be permitted ahead of the latter signal, or a train accepted from another direction in which there is no such additional home signal. Where switch diamonds are provided ahead of the junction home signal, after the additional home signal has been lowered for a train to proceed, the position of the switch diamonds must not be altered until the train has been brought to a stand at the junction home signal, or has passed clear of the switch diamonds.

Except where instructions are issued to the contrary, where a subsidiary signal is provided beneath the additional home signal this clause (f)(v) will not apply to the subsidiary signal.

The term 'junction' as used in this clause (f)(v) includes also connections through which a conflicting movement can be made.

(g) After a Wrong Line Order has been issued in accordance with Rule 184, permission must not be given for a train to occupy the line or approach from a box in rear, unless the train returning in the wrong direction can be diverted to another unoccupied line or into a siding for which the points have been set and the line can be kept clear for the train approaching in the proper direction in accordance with the conditions under which such train is to be accepted; nor must the line over which the wrong direction movement has been authorised be occupied or fouled by any other movement.

A Wrong Line Order must not be issued in accordance with Rule 184 after permission has been given for a train to occupy the line, or approach from a box in rear, unless the train to return in the wrong direction can be diverted to another unoccupied line or siding for which the points have been set, and the line can be kept clear for the train approaching in the proper direction in accordance with the conditions under which such train was accepted.

5. WARNING ARRANGEMENT (3-5-5)
(This bell signal must only be used as provided for in Regulations 4, 8, 9, and 14 and Rule 200, and where it is authorised by the Regional Operating Officer*. Except as provided in Regulations 4, 8, 9 and 14, and Rule 200, this Regulation must not be applied during fog and falling snow unless provided for in the special instructions.)
* Line Traffic Manager on the Eastern Region.

(a) When the line is clear to the home signal (or outermost home signal) only, the *Is line clear* signal must not be acknowledged in accordance with Regulation 1 but the *Warning Acceptance* signal (3-5-5) must be sent, and when this signal has been acknowledged the block indicator must be placed to the *Line clear* position. The Signalman receiving this signal must then deal with the train in accordance with Rule 41. When a train is drawing forward from the signalbox to the signal controlling the entrance to the section ahead and the *Warning Acceptance* signal is received, the signal must not be lowered until the train has been brought to a stand at it.

(b) If, before receipt of the *Train entering section* signal for a train which has been accepted under the *Warning Arrangement* in accordance with clause (a) the circumstances have so altered as to permit of the train being accepted under Regulation 4, the Signalman must send the bell signal 3-3-5 to the Signalman in rear, who must then understand that the line ahead of the home signal at the box in advance is now clear and that the fixed signals may be lowered for the train to proceed without being warned. The 3-3-5 signal must be acknowledged by repetition.

(c) In every case when a train is accepted under the *Warning Arrangement*, the Signalman in the rear must place a lever collar on the lever of the signal controlling the entrance to the section ahead to remind him that the signal must not be lowered until the arrangement laid down in clause (a) of this Regulation have been complied with, or the bell signal 3-3-5 has been received.

(d) Where the use of the *Warning Arrangement* is authorised, the *Train out of section* bell signal must be sent as soon as the train with tail lamp attached has arrived within the home signal train to be accepted under this Regulation, but the block indicator must remain at the *Train on line* position until the train has proceeded at a quarter of a mile beyond the home signal, or has been shunted clear of the running line, or until it is necessary to accept a following train under the *Warning Arrangement* in accordance with clause (a) of this Regulation. When the line is clear and no following train is being accepted under the *Warning Arrangement*, one beat on the bell must be sent to and acknowledged by the Signalman in the rear, after which the block indicator must be released from the *Train on line* position. The time the block indicator is released in accordance with this clause must be recorded in the train register at both boxes.

The Signalman at the box in rear may, after receiving the bell signal 2-1, offer the *Is line clear* signal for a train of the class authorised although the block indicator remains at the *Train on line* position.

6. TRAIN OUT OF SECTION (2-1)

(a) Except where instructions are issued to the contrary, or as shown in Regulations 5(d), a train must not be considered out of section and the *Train out of section* signal must not be sent and the block indicator placed to the normal position until the train with tail lamp attached has passed the signalbox and :-

(i) has passed at least a quarter of a mile beyond the outermost home signal, or

(ii) when the outermost home signal is situated at least a quarter of a mile in rear of the next home signal, the train has passed the latter signal, or

(iii) where instructions are given authorising a train to be accepted under Regulation 4 with the line clear for a distance other than a quarter of a mile beyond the outermost home signal, the train has passed beyond such special clearing point, or

(iv) has been shunted clear of the running line concerned, or

(v) at junctions when the train has passed well clear of the junction and the facing points have been set for another line which is clear in accordance with Regulation 4.

(b) When the last vehicle of a train does not pass the signalbox before it has been shunted into a siding, or when a train has been brought to a stand within the home signal, and it is necessary to send the *Train out of section* signal before the train passes the box, the Signalman must, before sending such signal, ascertain from the Guard or Shunter in charge of the train that the whole of the train, with tail lamp attached, has arrived, and the Guard or Shunter will be held responsible for giving this information to the Signalman; the Fireman will be similarly responsible in the case of a light engine.

(c) If an assisting engine or other vehicles are left on the running line within the clearing point, the *Train out of section* signal must not be sent until such vehicles have been shunted clear of the running line or have passed beyond the clearing point.

7. BLOCKING BACK

(A) Inside Home Signal (2-4).

(B) Outside Home Signal (3-3)

8. FREIGHT TRAIN, BALLAST TRAIN OR OFFICERS' SPECIAL TRAIN REQUIRING TO STOP IN SECTION (2-2-3). (SOUTHERN REGION 5 CONSECUTIVELY)

9. TROLLEY GOING INTO OR THROUGH TUNNELS (2-1-2) (SOUTHERN REGION 2-2-2)

10. ENGINE ASSISTING IN REAR OF TRAIN

11. ENGINE RUNNING ROUND ITS TRAIN

12. OBSTRUCTION DANGER (6 CONSECUTIVELY)

(a) In order to prevent the approach of a train when an obstruction occurs (or for other exceptional cause) the *Obstruction Danger* signal must be sent to the box in rear for the line or lines concerned, irrespective of whether or not the obstruction is within the clearing point or the *Is line clear* or *Train entering section* signal has been received from the box in rear. The *Obstruction Danger* signal need not be sent, however, if there are junction facing points which can be set for a direction which is clear of the obstruction and the line is clear in accordance with the Regulations. If it is necessary to alter such facing points in order to permit a train to pass over the junction from another direction and the obstruction is within the clearing point, it must first be protected by means of the *Blocking back inside home signal* signal.

The *Obstruction Danger* signal must also be sent to the box in rear when a Signalman observes or becomes aware of a train approaching his box for which he has:-

(i) not acknowledged the *Is line clear* signal;

(ii) not received the *Train entering section* signal;

(iii) not received the *Train or vehicles running away in right direction* signal, or

(iv) not acknowledged the *Shunting into forward section* signal.

Should a Signalman receive information which in his opinion necessitates the examination of the line or lines and no emergency bell signal has previously been sent or received, he must immediately comply with the provisions of this Regulation.

(b) The Signalman sending the *Obstruction Danger* signal must place the block indicator for the line or lines affected to, *Train on line*, if not already in that position, and must also place or maintain his signals at danger to protect the obstruction. He must then immediately telephone to the box to which the signal has been sent, explaining the reason for sending the signal.

The block indicator must be maintained at the *Train on line* position until the obstruction has been removed, except as provided in Regulation 14(b), and in Rule 198(b). When, however, the obstruction is ahead of the clearing point or the circumstances are such that a train can be passed clear of the obstruction, the Signalman may send the *Obstruction Removed* signal to the box in rear as soon as he has satisfied himself that it is safe to do so.

(c)(i) Should there be reason to suppose that both lines are affected, the Signalman must send the *Obstruction Danger* signal in both directions, and where there are adjoining running lines the requisite steps must be taken to stop trains approaching on any line or lines that may also be obstructed.

(ii) Should a Signalman observe or become aware that the advance section is obstructed he must advise the Signalman in advance of the circumstances so that he may act in accordance with this Regulation.

(d)(i) The Signalman receiving the *Obstruction Danger* signal must immediately place or maintain his signals at danger before acknowledging the signal and place 3 detonators, 10yd apart, on the obstructed line or lines in such a position as to prevent any train entering the obstructed section without passing over the detonators. He must not allow any train to proceed on the obstructed line or lines towards the signalbox from which he received the *Obstruction Danger* signal until he either receives the *Obstruction Removed* signal and the *Is line clear* signal has been acknowledged by the Signalman in advance, or it becomes necessary to allow a breakdown van train or other train to enter the section to render assistance. Such breakdown van train or other train going to render assistance must be signalled and dealt with in accordance with Regulation 14.

(ii) Where an emergency detonator placer is provided, this must also be operated for the obstructed line when the *Obstruction Danger* signal is received.

(e) Should a Signalman receiving the *Obstruction Danger* signal succeed in stopping a train for which the *Is line clear* signal has been acknowledged by the Signalman in advance, he must at once advise the Signalman at that box by sending the *Cancelling* signal (3-5). This signal must be acknowledged, but the block indicator must be maintained at the *Train on line* position until the obstruction has been removed as provided in clause (b) of this Regulation.

(f) Should a Signalman receiving the *Obstruction Danger* signal not be able to stop a train for which the *Is line clear* signal has been acknowledged by the Signalman in advance, or for which the *Train entering section* signal has been sent, he must, instead of acknowledging the *Obstruction Danger* signal, at once and without sending the *Call Attention* signal, send the *Train or vehicles running away in right direction* signal (4-5-5). The Signalman receiving the latter signal must immediately take all possible measures to stop the approaching train, and afterwards acknowledge the signal.

(g) When the obstruction has been removed and the line or lines are again clear, the *Obstruction Removed* signal must be sent to the box in rear and the block indicator placed or

Obstruction Removed signal must be sent to the box in rear and the block indicator placed or maintained at the normal position. Should, however, the Signalman in rear have been unable to stop a train for which the *Is line clear* signal has been acknowledged, the *Obstruction Removed* signal must not be sent to that box until such train is clear of the section.

(h) If after the *Obstruction Danger* signal has been sent it is necessary to ascertain which line or lines are obstructed an engine may be allowed to enter the section for this purpose at either end in accordance with Regulation 15.

13. ANIMALS ON LINE

14. SECTION OBSTRUCTED BY ACCIDENT OR BY DISABLED TRAIN

(a) Should a Signalman receive information from the Guard or Fireman of a disabled train standing in the section ahead or from the Signalman at the box in advance that a train is required to enter the section to assist the disabled train, or should it be necessary for a breakdown van train or Officers' Special to enter the section ahead which is obstructed by accident or otherwise, the assisting train or the breakdown van train or Officers' Special as the case may be, may, after having been brought to a stand and the Driver and Guard informed of the circumstances, be allowed to enter the section under the following arrangements:-

(i) The Signalman must inform the Signalman in advance of the circumstances, send the *Train entering section* signal to that box, and, after it has been acknowledged, note the circumstances in his train register. He may then allow the second train to enter the section and must instruct the Driver to pass at danger the signal controlling the entrance into the section ahead, as provided in Rule 38(b), and to proceed cautiously. The Signalman in advance must also note the circumstances in his train register, and must not send the *Train out of section* signal until both trains have arrived.

The Guard or Fireman of the train requiring assistance will ride on the engine of the second train, and point out to the Driver the position of the disabled train.

After the *Train out of section* signal has been received and permission obtained for another train to proceed, such train must be stopped at the box in rear, and the Driver instructed to proceed cautiously through the section.

(ii) Except during fog or falling snow, it will not be necessary for the Signalman in rear of the obstruction to detain the second train until the arrival at his box of the Guard or Fireman of the disabled train, if information has been received from the Signalman in advance that the Guard or Fireman is coming back. On receipt of this information the Signalman in rear may allow the second train to enter the obstructed section after the Driver has been informed that the Guard or Fireman of the disabled train is coming back, and has been instructed to keep a look-out for such Guard or Fireman.

During fog or falling snow, the second train must be detained at the signalbox, automatic stop signal, or semi-automatic stop signal worked automatically, in rear of the obstruction until the Guard or Fireman of the disabled train has arrived thereat, when he will so advise the Signalman.

(iii) If there is a tunnel in the obstructed section the second train must not enter such tunnel until the Guard or Fireman of the disabled train has come back and met the train or it has been ascertained that the tunnel is clear. The Driver of the second train must be instructed accordingly by the Signalman. The Signalman at each end of the section must stop any train proceeding on an adjoining line in the same or opposite direction and instruct the Driver to travel through the tunnel at reduced speed.

(iv) If the train, portion of train, or vehicle is removed from the section by being drawn back to the box in rear under the authority of the Wrong Line Order (form D) referred to in Rule 184, the block indicator must be maintained at the *Train on line* position, and when it has been ascertained that the line is again clear and the next train requires to pass over the line affected, the Signalman in rear must advise the Signalman in advance and send the *Train entering section* signal. When this signal has been acknowledged, the Signalman in the rear must inform the Driver what has occured and instruct him to proceed cautiously. the Driver must also be instructed to pass at danger the signal controlling the entrance into the section ahead, as provided in Rule 38(b). When the train with tail lamp attached has cleared the section in advance the Train out of section signal must be sent.

(b) When the line is clear to the outermost home signal, but is occupied by a train or otherwise obstructed ahead of that signal, and assistance is required from the rear, the Signalman in rear must be informed of the circumstances. Should a train have stopped within the authorised clearing point and require assistance, provided it has arrived with tail lamp attached, the *Train out of section* bell signal only must be sent to enable the assisting train to be offered and accepted in accordance with Regulation 5. If the *Obstruction Danger* signal has been sent for an obstruction in advance of the authorised clearing point, the *Obstruction Removed* signal must be sent and the assisting train then accepted. If, however, the obstruction is within the authorised clearing point, the 2-1 bell signal only must be sent but the block indicator maintained at the *Train on line* position until the assisting train is offered; such train may be accepted under Regulation 5. The Driver of the second train must be verbally informed by the Signalman at the box in rear of the circumstances existing at the box in advance.

When the line is clear to the outermost home signal but is occupied by a train or is otherwise obstructed ahead of that signal and it is necessary to work a train forward to a point in rear of the obstruction, such a train must be dealt with in accordance with the arrangement outlined in the preceding paragraph.

(c) Should it be necessary for the assisting train to continue in rear of the disabled train through any block section or sections in advance of the section obstructed, the Signalman in rear, when sending the *Is line clear* signal for the disabled train, or if this signal has already been sent, must inform the Signalman in advance that the approaching train is being assisted in rear by a train or engine, and the Signalman receiving this information must enter it in the train register and must not send the *Train out of section* signal until both trains have arrived.

(d) Where a train becomes disabled in section and a Signalman receives information of the fact from either the Fireman of the disabled train or the Signalman in rear he may, if necessary, occupy or foul the line ahead of the outermost home signal for that line on which the disabled train was approaching until such time as the second train is ready to enter from the box in rear in accordance with clause (a)(i). The *Train entering section* signal for the second train must not be acknowledged until the line at the box in advance is again clear in accordance with the conditions which existed when the disabled train was accepted.

(e) In the event of a train, portion of train, or vehicle being removed from the section by an engine admitted from the box in advance, the Signalman at such box must advise the Signalman at the box in rear of the circumstances. When the train, portion of train, or vehicle is removed, whether at the rear or the advance end of the section, and the section is clear, the block indicator must be maintained at *Train on line* and the next train required to pass over the line affected must be dealt with in accordance with clause (a)(iv) of this Regulation.

15. EXAMINATION OF LINE

(a) When it is necessary, in accordance with Regulations 12, 16, 17, 19, 20, 22 and 23, to ascertain if a line or lines are clear, an engine may be allowed to enter the section for the purpose on any other line used by trains in the same or opposite direction provided telephone communication exists between the two boxes, which will admit of a proper understanding being arrived at between the two Signalmen, and the *Train out of section* signal, or the bell signal 2-1 in accordance with Regulation 5(d), has been received for the previous train. In connection with clauses (c) and (d) of this Regulation (15), the engine may be allowed to travel through the section over any line.

If the line ahead of the outermost home signal of the box in advance is occupied by a train, the bell signal 2-1 may be sent to enable an engine to enter the section for examination of the line, but the block indicator must be maintained at the *Train on line* position.

The circumstances must be explained to the Driver and he must be instructed to pass at danger the signal controlling the entrance into the section ahead as provided in Rule 38(b), and proceed cautiously through the section, prepared to stop short of any obstruction. Where practicable the engine must be accompanied by a Station Master or other competent person. After sunset, during fog or falling snow, or where a tunnel intervenes, the engine must always be so accompanied.

(b) The Signalman at the box at which the engine enters the section must not send the *Is line clear* signal but must inform the Signalman in advance of the circumstances under which the engine is entering the section, and the *Train entering section* signal must be sent and acknowledged. The block indicator must be placed or maintained at *Train on line* until the engine has arrived at the box in advance or has returned to the box in rear and the person accompanying the engine, or the Driver, as the case may be, has reported which line or lines are safe for the passage of trains. Should the engine return in the wrong direction under the authority of a Wrong Line Order (form A, B or D) and the line is safe for the passage of trains the *Cancelling* signal (3-5) must be sent.

After arrangements have been made for an engine to enter the section in accordance with this clause, the Signalman in advance may occupy the line ahead of the home signal, but should the engine return to the box in rear and the Cancelling signal be received, the *Blocking Back* signal (2-4) must immediately be sent and acknowledged, as provided for in Regulation 7(A) if the line ahead of the home signal is occupied.

(c) In connection with Regulation 12(h), if it is necessary for an engine to enter the section at the box in rear on the affected line, the Signalman who sent the *Obstruction Danger* signal may, after coming to a clear understanding with the Signalman at the box in rear, and provided the adjoining line or lines are not occupied between the two boxes concerned, send the *Obstruction Removed* signal, but the block indicator must be maintained at the *Train on line* position.

After permission has been given for an engine to enter the section on the affected line, no train must be allowed to enter the section on the adjoining line or lines until it is known that it is safe to do so.

(d) In connection with Regulation 17, for the purpose of ascertaining if the line or lines are clear, an engine may, in accordance with the instructions laid down in clauses (a) and (b) of this Regulation (15), be allowed to enter the sections, both in rear and in advance of the signalbox from which the *Stop and examine train* signal was sent, on the same line and in the same direction as the train concerned has proceeded, provided the *Train out of section* signal has been received for the train. If the line is clear to the home signal only, the *Train out of section* or *Obstruction Removed* bell signal must, when necessary, be sent to the Signalman at the box in rear to enable the engine to be signalled as shown in clause (b), but the block indicator must be maintained at the *Train on line* position.

If definite information is received that a passenger has fallen from a train and it is necessary for the line to be examined, a brake van (coaching or freight), in which a Guard must ride, may be attached in rear of an engine for the purpose of examining the line, but the Signalman at the box in advance must be advised accordingly. When the Station Master, or other competent person, is accompanying the engine and brake van, he must ride on the engine. A passenger train or other train composed of coaching stock or a freight train with automatic brake operative on not less than one third of the vehicles may also be allowed to enter the section for this purpose on the same or any other line provided it is daylight, the weather is clear and that no tunnel intervenes. the train must be dealt with as laid down in the third paragraph of clause (e) of this Regulation.

(e) In connection with Regulations 19 or 20, when it is required to ascertain if the line is clear after the divided train or front portion thereof has arrived, a train may be allowed to enter the section on an adjoining line for the purpose, provided the weather is clear and no tunnel intervenes on the line over which the divided train or portion thereof has travelled.

If catch points exist in the line over which the divided train or portion thereof has travelled, the Signalman must advise the Driver and other person who may be riding with him that the train must be stopped short of the catch points and not allowed to proceed until it has been ascertained the line in the vicinity of the catch points is not obstructed, if necessary an examination on foot being made. Where catch points exist a train conveying passengers may, however, be allowed to enter the section only during daylight.

The Signalman at the box where the train enters the section must advise the Signalman in advance by telephone the description of the train, which must then be signalled, accompanied and otherwise dealt with as laid down in clauses (a) and (b) for an engine. The line ahead of the home signal at the box in advance must not, however, be occupied as provided in the second paragraph of clause (b) unless authority is given for the class of train so used to approach that box under normal working in accordance with Regulation 5.

(f) For the purposes of this Regulation a multiple-unit electric or diesel train not conveying passengers, or a unit of a train of this type from which any passengers have been detrained, may be regarded as an engine and such train or portion thereof must be dealt with in the same way as an engine. The Signalman at the box in advance must, however, be advised as to whether a train, a unit of a train, or an engine, is entering the section.

16. TRAIN AN UNUSUALLY LONG TIME IN SECTION (6-2)

17. STOP AND EXAMINE TRAIN (7 CONSECUTIVELY)

(a) Signalmen must be careful to notice each train as it passes to ascertain whether there is any apparent necessity for having it stopped at the next signalbox for examination.

If a Signalman observes or becomes aware of anything unusual in a train during its passage, such as signals of alarm, goods falling off, a vehicle on fire, a hot axle-box, or other mishap (except a tail lamp missing, a tail light out, or a train divided, for which see Regulation 19 and 20), he must, after the *Train entering section* signal has been acknowledged, send to the Signalman in advance the Stop and examine train signal. He must also exhibit his signals to prevent any train from proceeding on the line used in the opposite direction except when he is satisfied that such line is not affected; if, after a train on the opposite line has been stopped, the Signalman has reason to believe that such line is not affected, the train may be allowed to proceed after the Driver has been advised of the circumstances. the Signalman in advance must also be advised of the reason for sending the *Stop and examine train* signal.

(b) The Signalman in advance must immediately exhibit his signals to stop the train coming from the signalbox from which the signal was received and any train going towards that box on the opposite line. The train for which the signal was received, when stopped, must be carefully examined and dealt with as occasion may require. If it is not possible to detach the vehicle in respect of which the emergency bell signal was sent, or to rectify the defect, or otherwise deal with the emergency, and it is considered that the train may be allowed to proceed with safety to a signalbox in advance where the matter can be dealt with as occasion may require, the train must be signalled forward in the usual way, the *Stop and examine train* signal being sent immediately the acknowledgement of the *Train entering section* signal is received. The train must not, however, be allowed to proceed until any train on the opposite or adjoining line has passed clear of the train concerned.

Should the Signalman who received the *Stop and examine train* signal be able to ascertain from the trainmen after the examination of the train that the opposite line is not obstructed, he may allow trains to proceed. Should, however, he be unable to ascertain any reason for the signal being sent, he must inform the Driver of the first train travelling on the opposite line of the circumstances, and instruct him to proceed cautiously to the next signalbox. In either case, before a train is allowed to proceed, the Signalman who sent the *Stop and examine train* signal must be advised of the circumstances.

(c) Should either Signalman become aware or have reason to believe that the permanent way is fouled or damaged, he must immediately advise the Signalman at the opposite end of the section or sections affected, the provisions of Regulation 12 being carried out as necessary. No train except as laid down in Regulation 15(d), second paragraph, must be allowed to proceed through such section or sections affected in the same or opposite direction in accordance with Regulation 15.

(d) Should the *Stop and examine train* signal have been sent on account of a door being open on a passenger train, the Signalman sending the signal must advise the Signalman in rear, and trains running on the same or opposite line between these signalboxes need not be detained to await evidence that the line is not obstructed but the first train in each direction must be stopped, the Driver informed of the circumstances and instructed to proceed cautiously to the next signalbox, keeping a good look out. If, however, the section is short and the signalman can satisfy themselves by observation that it is clear, it will not be necessary for trains to be cautioned.

If information is received that a passenger has fallen from the train, the Signalman concerned must act in accordance with clause (c).

(e) The *Stop and examine train* signal must always be sent in any of the circumstances named, even where in short sections a train may have passed into the forward section.

If the Signalman receiving the *Stop and examine train* signal cannot stop the train, he must immediately pass on the signal to the Signalman in advance.

18. MAINTENANCE OF ABSOLUTE BLOCK SIGNALLING DURING SINGLE LINE WORKING

Should any obstruction occur necessitating single line working, Absolute Block signalling must be maintained whenever possible, but should it be necessary to suspend Absolute Block signalling the provisions of Rule 198 must be observed. When Absolute Block signalling is suspended the authority for the suspension is cancelled by the withdrawal of the Single Line Working forms.

19. TRAIN PASSED WITHOUT TAIL LAMP (9 CONSECUTIVELY TO BOX IN ADVANCE, 4-5 TO BOX IN REAR)

(a) Signalmen must carefully watch each train as it passes, and satisfy themselves that it is complete with tail lamp attached before sending the *Train out of section* signal.

(b) Should a train pass without a tail lamp, or the Signalman be unable to satisfy himself whether or not the tail lamp is on the train, he must immediately place or maintain his signals at danger to stop the first train proceeding on the opposite line, and except as provided in clause (d), inform the Driver what has occurred and instruct him to proceed cautiously so as to avoid danger in the event of any portion of the train having fouled the line on which his train is running. The Signalman must also send the *Train passed without tail lamp* signal (9 consecutive beats) to the box in advance; he must not send the *Train out of section* signal to the box in rear, but must send the *Train passed without tail lamp* signal (4-5) and maintain the block indicator at *Train on line.* Should he afterwards receive the *Train out of section* signal from the box in advance or be advised by the Signalman at that box that the train is complete, he must send the *Train out of section* signal to the box in rear, but should it be ascertained that the train is divided the provisions of Regulation 20 (so far as they apply) must be carried out.

(c) The Signalman in advance on receiving the *Train passed without tail lamp* signal must immediately place or maintain his signals at danger to stop the approaching train, and ascertain whether or not the train is complete. If the train is complete he must advise the Signalman in rear, unless he is in a position to send the *Train out of section* signal. If the train is incomplete he must advise the Signalman in rear accordingly.

If, where the sections are short, a Signalman receiving the *Train passed without tail lamp* signal (9 consecutive beats) finds that he cannot stop the train except by bringing it to a sudden stand, he must not place his signals to danger, but, as the train is approaching, send the *Train entering section* signal to the box in advance and immediately follow it with the *Train passed without tail lamp* signal. In these circumstances it will not be necessary for him to send the *Train passed without tail lamp* signal (4-5) to the box in rear or to stop the first train on the opposite line.

(d) Should a train pass without a tail lamp and there is a tunnel in rear, or during fog or falling snow, no train (except an engine as provided for in Regulation 15) must be allowed to enter the section on either line until it has been ascertained that the line on which it is about to run is not obstructed. If there are catch points in the section, the provisions of Regulation 15(e) must be carried out.

(e) Should a freight train pass without tail lamp and also without side lamps the Signalman must assume that the train has become divided. He must send the *Train Divided* signal (5-5) to the box in advance unless he has reason to believe that the second portion will not enter the advance section, in which case the *Stop and examine train* signal (7 consecutive beats) must be sent. He must, in addition, send the *Train passed without tail lamp* signal (4-5) to the box in rear and advise the Signalman of the reason for the signal being sent. If, however, there is a rising gradient in the section from the box in rear, the Signalman must carry out the provisions of Regulation 22, in which case it will not be necessary for the 4-5 signal to be sent.

The Signalman receiving the 4-5 signal in these circumstances must stop any trains from going towards the box from which the signal was received.

NOTE — This clause is not applicable to Class 'C' (fully fitted) freight trains except in the Southern Region.

(f) Where the Signalman is authorised to send the *Train out of section* signal before the train has passed the box and he subsequently becomes aware that a train is without a tail lamp, he must carry out the provisions of Regulation 12 or 22, according to the circumstances, in respect of the rear section.

(g) Should a train pass with a tail light out when it should be burning, and the Signalman can plainly see the lamp and is satisfied that the train is complete, or should a freight train pass with side lamp missing when it should be exhibited or with side light out when it should be burning or with incorrect side light or lamp exhibited, the Signalman must send the *Train out of section* signal to the box in rear, and the *Train passed without tail lamp* signal (9 consecutive beats) to the box in advance, and where applicable, also advise the Signalman in advance of the circumstances. In such a case it will not be necessary for the Signalman sending the signal to stop a train on the opposite line.

20. TRAIN DIVIDED (5-5)

(a) The *Train Divided* signal must be sent to the signalbox in advance whenever a train which has become divided is entering, or is likely to enter, the section ahead in two or more portions, also as provided in Regulation 19(e). The Signalman sending the *Train Divided* signal must immediately stop any train travelling in the same or opposite direction on any other line.

(b) The Signalman receiving the *Train Divided* signal must stop any train travelling in the opposite direction, and if expedient in the circumstances, also stop any train travelling in the same direction on any line.

(c) If the divided train:-
    (i) is assisted by an engine in rear, or
    (ii) is running on a falling gradient or where the line is level or between short sections, where the stopping of the first portion would risk a collision with the second portion, the Signalman, provided permission had been obtained from the box in advance for the train to proceed, must not stop the first portion, but must exhibit to the Driver a green handsignal waved slowly from side to side.

    In such circumstances, should the Signalman receiving the *Train Divided* signal have reason to think he may be unable to stop the rear portion of the divided train, he must send forward the *Train Divided* signal on receipt.

(d) If the Signalman considers that the stopping of the first portion would cause a collision with the second portion and he has been unable to obtain permission for the divided train to proceed to the box in advance, he may, by the exhibition of a green handsignal waved slowly from side to side, authorise the Driver of the first portion to pass at danger the signal controlling the entrance of trains to the section ahead for the purpose of avoiding or reducing the force of a collision, provided:-
    (i) there is a rising gradient in the section ahead sufficiently long or steep to bring the second portion to a stand, and the Signalman considers that the time which has elapsed since the previous train passed his box makes it safe to do so; or
    (ii) the weather is clear, there is no tunnel in the section, no passenger train has been accepted in the opposite direction on any adjoining line, and the Signalman considers that the time which has elapsed since the previous train passed his box makes it safe to do so.

In either case the provisions of the first paragraph of Rule 39(a) will not apply.

    If the first portion is being allowed to enter the section ahead under either of these conditions, the Signalman in advance must be immediately advised of the circumstances and the *Train entering section* signal must be sent. The Signalman in advance on receipt of this advise must immediately place or maintain his signals at danger to prevent any train proceeding towards the box from which the advice was received. If the second portion enters the section ahead the *Train Divided* signal must also be sent.

(e) If the conditions of clauses (c) or (d) do not apply, the first portion must not be allowed to enter the section ahead. Where possible it must be disposed of expeditiously in an endeavour to prevent the second portion coming into collision with it.

(f) In the circumstances described in clauses (c), (d) and (e) the Signalman must as soon as the first portion of the train has passed or otherwise been dealt with, place or maintain the signals at danger and take proper measures for dealing with the second portion, placing detonators on the rail and exhibiting a red handsignal to attract the attention of the trainmen.

(g) Should a train become divided in starting and the first portion proceed, leaving the rear portion stationary, the *Stop and examine train* signal (7 consecutive beats) must be sent to the box in advance, and not the *Train Divided* signal. Should the second portion of a train which has become divided in running, come to a stand before entering the section in advance, the *Stop and examine train* signal must be sent provided the *Train Divided* signal has not already been sent.

In either case the Signalman must inform the Signalman at the box in advance of the circumstances (also if necessary the Signalman at the box in the rear), and arrange for the first portion to be stopped.

(h) When it is necessary to remove a portion of a train or a vehicle from a section, the provisions of Regulation 14 must be observed.

(i) Should any train travelling in the opposite direction, or in the same direction on any line, have been stopped, it must not, except as provided in Regulation 15(e), be allowed to proceed until it has been ascertained that the line on which it is about to run is not obstructed. A light engine may, however, be allowed to enter the section in accordance with Regulation 15, clauses (a) and (b).

Should, however, the rearmost portion of a divided rain arrive within the home signal at the box in advance complete with tail lamp and accompanied by the Guard, the Signalman may, after ascertaining from the Guard that the rear portion is intact and so informing the Signalman in rear, send the *Train out of section* signal in accordance with Regulation 6, but the first train requiring to travel over the adjoining line in the opposite direction must be stopped and the Driver informed of the circumstances and instructed to proceed cautiously.

(j) If it is necessary for a train to follow the first portion of a train which has become divided, such train must not be allowed to enter the section until the Signalman at each end is satisfied that the section is clear. The Signalman in rear must then advise the Signalman in advance of the train which is about to enter the section and send the *Train entering section* signal. When this signal has been acknowledged he must inform the Driver of what has occured, and instruct him to pass at danger the signal controlling the entrance into the section ahead as provided in Rule 38(b), and to proceed cautiously. On the train arriving at the box in advance, with tail lamp attached, the *Train out of section* signal must be sent in accordance with Regulation 6. the same course must be adopted if the second portion of the divided train is worked through the section ahead, immediately following the first portion.

21. SHUNT TRAIN FOR FOLLOWING TRAIN TO PASS (1-5-5)

22. TRAIN OR VEHICLES RUNNING AWAY IN WRONG DIRECTION (2-5-5)

(a) Should any train, portion of a train, or a vehicle, be running back in the wrong direction, or a train proceed without authority on a line in the wrong direction, the Signalman must immediately place or maintain the signals at danger on any line which may be affected, send the *Train or vehicles running away in wrong direction* signal to the box towards which the train or vehicles are running and place the block indicator for the line affected to *Train on line* if it is not already in that position. The first train going in the same direction as the runaway vehicles must not be allowed to proceed until it has been ascertained that the line is not obstructed, but an engine may be allowed to enter the section in accordance with Regulation 15.

(b) The Signalman receiving this signal must immediately stop any train going towards the signalbox from which the signal was received, and take any other measures that may be necessary, such as turning the runaway train or vehicles across to the right line or into a siding, and stopping any train coming from the box from which the signal was received, if expedient under the circumstances. In the event of a runaway train or vehicles being turned across to the right line the *Train or vehicles running away in right direction* signal (4-5-5) must be sent to the next signalbox towards which the train or vehicles are running.

If the Signalman receiving the *Train or vehicles running away in wrong direction* signal is unable to take any such protective measures he must send the signal to the next box in rear; he must also place detonators on the line.

(c) No train must be allowed to proceed over the line for which the 2-5-5 signal was sent until it has been ascertained that the line is clear. Should the runaway train or vehicles stop in section and be removed by being propelled forward to the box in advance, the provisions of Regulation 14(a)(i) must be observed. If, however, the train or vehicles travel through the section to the box in rear, or are removed from the section other than in accordance with Regulation 14(a)(i) the block indicator must be maintained at the *Train on line* position and the next train requiring to pass over the line affected must be dealt with in accordance with Regulation 14(a)(iv).

23. TRAIN OR VEHICLES RUNNING AWAY IN RIGHT DIRECTION (4-5-5)

(a) If any train, portion of a train, or a vehicle, is running away in the right direction on the proper line, or has entered the section without authority, the Signalman must send the *Train or vehicles running away in right direction* signal to the box in advance. The Signalman sending this signal must immediately stop any train going in the direction of the box towards which the runaway train or vehicle is running, and, if expedient in the circumstances, must also stop any train on the opposite line or lines.

(b) The Signalman receiving the signal must place or maintain the block indicator at the *Train on line* position and immediately stop any train from going towards the box from which the signal was received. He must place or maintain the signals at danger against the runaway train or vehicles, arrange for the line on which it is running to be cleared, and if expedient send the signal forward unless the runaway train or vehicle can be diverted from the running line; he must also place detonators on the rails and take such other measures as may be most expedient under the circumstances.

Should, however, there be a train in the section in front of the runaway train or vehicles, the train in front must, if the line is clear, be allowed to pass, after which the signals must be immediately exhibited against the runaway train. In these circumstances, the *Train or vehicles running away in right direction* signal must not be sent forward as described in the preceding paragraph, until the train in front has passed into the section ahead, if such train is proceeding on the same line as that on which the runaway train or vehicle may follow.

No train must be allowed to proceed through the section in the same or opposite direction until it has been ascertained that the line concerned is not obstructed, but an engine may be allowed to enter the section in accordance with Regulation 15.

(c) If the *Train or vehicles running away in right direction* signal is received during the time the section is unoccupied and the train or portion of the train arrives complete with tail lamp attached, the *Train out of section* signal must be sent.

If the *Train or vehicles running away in right direction* signal is received during the time the section is occupied by another train the *Train out of section* signal must not be sent until both the train occupying the section and the runaway train or vehicles with tail lamp attached have passed out of the section. The next following train must be signalled in the usual way, and after permission has been obtained for such train to proceed cautiously through the section.

Should the train or portion of train arrive without a tail lamp, the Signalman must so inform the Signalman in rear, and the block indicator must be maintained at the *Train on line* position. When both signalmen are satisfied that the line is clear the next train to pass over the line affected must be dealt with in accordance with clause (d) of this Regulation.

(d) Should the runaway train or vehicles stop in section and be removed by being propelled forward to the box in advance, the provisions of Regulation 14(a)(i) must be observed.

If, however, the train or vehicles are removed from the section other than in accordance with Regulation 14(a)(i) the block indicator must be maintained at the *Train on line* position and the next train requiring to pass over the line affected must be dealt with in accordance with Regulation 14(a)(iv).

24. OPENING AND CLOSING OF SIGNALBOXES

25. FAILURE OF BLOCK SIGNALLING APPARATUS

In the event of a failure of block signalling apparatus so that trains cannot be block-signalled in the ordinary way, steps must be taken immediately to have the apparatus put into working order and the following instructions observed in the meantime:-

(a)(i) Except as provided in clause (h) a train must not in any circumstances be allowed to pass a box into the section where the failure exists without having been previously brought to a stand and the Driver and the rear Guard, also the Driver of an engine assisting in rear, if any, advised of the failure. Should there be no bell or telephone communication with the box in advance trainmen must, in addition, be advised of this to enable the provisions of Rule 56 to be complied with. The Driver or Drivers must also be instructed to pass at danger the signal controlling the entrance to the section ahead in accordance with Rule 38(b), and to proceed cautiously.

When a Driver has been stopped at a box and advised by the Signalman of the failure, the Driver must be instructed to draw his train forward and bring it again to a stand with the brake van near to the box to enable the Signalman to verbally inform the rear Guard, and the Driver of an engine assisting in rear, if any, of the failure; the Driver of the train engine must also be told that, after this has been done, he must not start again until he receives a green handsignal from the Signalman.

(ii) The Signalman at whose box the block instruments and/or bells have failed must advise the Signalman at the opposite end of the section concerned of the failure, by telephone. Where telephone communication is not available, the Signalman at the box in rear must instruct the Driver of the first train that is being cautioned to stop at the box in advance and inform the Signalman of the circumstances.

(iii) When the bells only, or bells and block instruments, have failed and a telephone is available, the Signalman must send the necessary bell signals as messages on the telephone,

for example:-

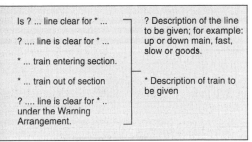

Is ? ... line clear for * ...	? Description of the line to be given; for example: up or down main, fast, slow or goods.
? .... line is clear for * ...	
* ... train entering section.	
* ... train out of section	* Description of train to be given
? .... line is clear for * .. under the Warning Arrangement.	

A Signalman sending signals in this manner must satisfy himself that he is speaking to the Signalman who should receive the communication.

When the bells have failed but the block instruments are still available, these must be worked in conjunction with the telephone messages.

When the block instruments only have failed, the bell signals must be sent in accordance with these Regulations.

A train must not be allowed to enter the section until permission has been received from the Signalman in advance in accordance with these Regulations.

(iv) When the bells have failed and telephone communication is not available, a train must not be allowed to follow another train until the time usually taken by the preceding train to clear the section, after allowing for the train having been stopped, has elapsed, but in no case with an interval less than three minutes. Where there is a tunnel in the section, an interval of not less than 10 minutes must be allowed between two trains, unless the Signalman can satisfy himself that the tunnel is clear.

(v) In the event of a failure as described in paragraph (iii) applying to one line only, the normal signalling of trains must be maintained on the adjoining line or lines the block apparatus for which is in working order, but the Driver of the first train travelling on each such adjoining line or lines must be advised of the circumstances and instructed to proceed cautiously through the section.

In cases where trains on one line have to be worked in accordance with paragraph (iv), all trains on the adjoining line or lines must be stopped and the Driver of each train instructed to proceed cautiously. Trains, other than the first, on an adjoining line need not, however, be stopped and cautioned when the failure occurs on a line not worked in accordance with the Absolute Block Regulations.

(vi) When trains are signalled in accordance with paragraph (iii), all signals sent or received on the bell or telephone must be recorded whether the ordinary block signals are usually recorded or not, and when trains are being worked in accordance with paragraph (iv), the departure time of each train must be recorded.

(b)(i) Where trains are being worked in accordance with clause (a)(iv) and the telephone or bells are restored the Driver of the next train allowed to proceed through the section over the line or lines on which the failure exists must, when being cautioned, be supplied with a ticket which he must be instructed to hand to the Signalman at the next box in advance, intimating that the train carrying the ticket will be the last train to pass through the section in accordance with clause (a)(iv) and that, on receipt of this ticket, the working will then be in accordance with clause (a)(iii). On receipt of this ticket the *Train out of section* signal must be sent for that train in accordance with the conditions of Regulation 6. The Signalman in rear must not offer a following train until this signal has been received.

(ii) When all the apparatus is in working order and has been tested in accordance with Regulation 26, the Driver of the next train allowed to proceed through the section over the line or lines on which the failure existed must be cautioned and supplied with a ticket intimating that the train carrying this ticket will be the last train cautioned through the section, and he must be instructed to stop at the box in advance and hand this ticket to the Signalman. The Signalman receiving this ticket must send the *Train out of section* signal in accordance with Regulation 6, and the ordinary method of signalling must be resumed. Particulars of the failure must be reported on the appropriate form without delay.

(iii) When the train is worked by two engines in front or assisted by an engine or engines in rear the ticket must be shown to all Drivers on the train, and carried by the rearmost Driver.

(c) When a box which has been switched out of circuit is being opened the Signalman must be advised by the Signalman on each side, by telephone or other means, that the block instruments or bells are out of order, or that a failure has been remedied but normal working has not been resumed. The Signalman so advised must act in accordance with clause (a) or (b) as may be necessary. If trains are being worked in accordance with clause (a)(iv), the Signalman on each side of an intermediate box due to open must not decrease the existing time interval between trains until it is definitely ascertained that the box has been opened.

(d) Should the Driver of the first train that arrives at a signalbox after it has been opened, produce a ticket showing that the block instruments and bells have been out of order during the time the box has been closed, and that the failure has been remedied, the Driver (if the block instruments and bells of the section in advance are in working order) must be instructed to take the ticket forward to the next box. After the train has cleared the section in rear of the box which has been opened, the *Train out of section* signal must be sent in accordance with Regulation 6.

(e) A signalbox may be closed before the failure of the instruments or bells has been rectified, but the Station Master's permission must, when practicable, be obtained. When the box is due to be closed the following procedure must be adopted:-

(i) If the *closing* bell signal cannot be sent but telephone communication is available, this must be used to advise the Signalman on each side that the box is about to be closed.

(ii) When the Closing bell signal cannot be sent and telephone communication is not available, the Signalman must send a written message to the next box open on each side of him, but the signals must not be lowered (where block switches are provided) nor the Signalman leave duty until the usual time has elapsed for the train which last passed his box to pass through the section. A passing train may be used to convey the written message. The Signalman on each side of the box due to close must on receipt of this message increase the time interval accordingly.

(iii) When the last train for the day has passed, communication with the boxes on each side may be dispensed with, and if the failure has not been remedied by the time traffic is resumed the method of working as set out in clause (a) must again be adopted.

(iv) The circumstances must be noted by the Signalman in the train register and, in addition, he must leave a notice, suitably worded, in a conspicuous position for the information of the Signalman next on duty.

Where, however, the signals controlling the entrance to the section ahead are controlled by *Line clear* on the block instruments, the signal box must remain in circuit until the fault is remedied or the line is closed to traffic.

(f) When the block instruments or bells fail and there is a level crossing in the section provided with block indicators or bells, but which is not a block post, the Signalman, if telephone communication with the crossing is available, must inform the person in charge of the crossing that the block indicators or bells are not in working order. If there is no telephone communication with the crossing, or the telephone has failed, the Signalman must instruct the Driver of every train proceeding in the direction of the crossing during the failure to approach the level crossing cautiously, sound the engine whistle and be prepared to stop short of any obstruction at such crossing. The time interval must also be extended sufficiently to allow for the additional time likely to be occupied in carrying out this instruction.

(g) When trains are being worked in accordance with clause (a)(iv), all trains must be brought within the protection of the home signal as promptly as possible, and to obviate a train standing with its rear portion outside the home signal, the Signalman must, if necessary, authorise the Driver to draw forward a sufficient distance to bring the rear portion within the home signal.

If a train requires to stand outside a home signal for the purpose of attaching or detaching traffic, or through any other cause, the Signalman must, if practicable, obtain the assistance of a Handsignalman provided with the necessary detonators and handsignals, who must be sent out a sufficient distance from the rear of the train to afford protection. Until this Handsignalman has been provided, a train must not be stopped outside the home signal to attach or detach traffic.

(h) In the event of the first portion of a divided train being required to enter the section ahead in accordance with Regulation 20, clause (c) or (d), during a failure of the block instruments or bells it will not be necessary for the Driver to be advised of the failure or cautioned as laid down in this Regulation (25), neither will it be necessary for the first portion of the train to be detained until the interval of time prescribed in clause (a)(iv), has elapsed. The provisions of the last paragraph of clause (d) of Regulation must, however, be carried out as far as practicable.

26. TESTING BLOCK INDICATORS AND BELLS (16 CONSECUTIVELY)

27. ADDITIONAL RUNNING LINES

28. LEVEL CROSSINGS

29. MIXED TRAINS

30. BREAKDOWN VAN TRAIN, AND ENGINE REPLACING OR ASSISTING DISABLED ENGINE

31. SHUNTING INTO FORWARD SECTION (3-3-2)
(This Regulation will only apply where authorised by the Regional Operating Officer — Line Traffic Manager on the Eastern Region.)

(a) A train must not be allowed to pass into the section ahead for shunting purposes until the signal *Shunting into forward section* (3-3-2) has been sent to and acknowledged by the Signalman in advance.

(b) The Signalman in advance, on receipt of this signal must, if the line is clear to the outermost home signal, acknowledge it by repetition and place the block indicator to *Train on line* if not already in that position.
(c) After the Driver has been verbally instructed as to what is required to be done the signal

controlling the entrance to the section ahead must then be lowered for the train to draw forward towards the box in advance. Where a shunt-ahead signal is provided below such signal this must be used instead of verbal instructions to the Driver.

Where the signal controlling the entrance to the section ahead is controlled by the block indicator and a shunt-ahead signal is not provided, the Signalman in advance after acknowledging the *Shunting into forward section* signal, must place the block indicator to the *Line clear* position to enable the signal controlling the entrance to the section ahead to be lowered and, after the Signalman in rear has lowered such signal and the train is ready to draw forward, he must send *Train entering section* signal to the box in advance, which signal must be acknowledged in accordance with Regulation 1.

(d) When the operation is completed the *Shunt withdrawn* signal (8 consecutively) must be sent to the Signalman in advance who must acknowledge the signal by repetition and act as follows:

(i) If the block indicator was in the normal position at the time the *Shunting into forward section* signal (3-3-2) was acknowledged, replace the block indicator to normal, unless the line ahead of the outermost home signal has been occupied in the meantime, in which case the provisions of Regulation 7(A) must be carried out.

(ii) If the block indicator was in the *Train on line* position when the 3-3-2 signal was acknowledged and the line at his box has become clear in the meantime, send the 2-1 bell signal and place the block indicator to normal.

(iii) If the block indicator was in the *Train on line* position when the 3-3-2 signal was acknowledged and the line at his box remains obstructed, maintain the block indicator at *Train on line*.

32. WORKING IN WRONG DIRECTION (2-3-3)

Left:
Standard upper quadrants with slightly shorter than standard enamelled arms, photographed at New Holland Town on the ex-MS&LR. The board on the signalbox immediately behind the signals, displays the numbers of the levers which operate the arms.